COMIC BOOKS
AND OTHER HOOKS:
21st Century Education

COMIC BOOKS
AND OTHER HOOKS:
21st Century Education

Dear Mr. and Mrs. Pereira
Thank you for giving me
my start and for always being
there ... A fact I will
Never forget. (See dedications)

Manfred J. von Vulte

authorHOUSE®

AuthorHouse™ LLC
1663 Liberty Drive
Bloomington, IN 47403
www.authorhouse.com
Phone: 1-800-839-8640

Published by AuthorHouse 12/20/2013

ISBN: 978-1-4918-4625-4 (sc)
ISBN: 978-1-4918-4623-0 (hc)
ISBN: 978-1-4918-4624-7 (e)

Library of Congress Control Number: 2013923327

Table of Contents

Dedication and Thanks

To my wife, Charmaine von Vulte, you make it all possible.
To my son Robert and those to follow, you are the future.

Mrs. D. von Vulte (Mother)
John and Susan Leitmann
Golding and Wong Families
Peter and Stacey Leitmann, Dear Kateri
Karl and Rocio Leitmann, Dear Tristan and Mateya
William Leitmann
Talya Leitmann
Rosemarie Leitmann and Andrew Kemp
Nicollete and Anastasia Kemp
H.J. von Vulte
Heidi von Vulte and Mark Kuhne
Dr. Gerhard Schormann and Family
Uncle Edmund Schormann
John Hess and Family
Grant Zagol, Alvin Sumilang, Charles Sue-Wah-Sing
Andrew Kim R.I.P.
Gene and Michelle Ascenzi, Dan and Alana Cameron
Patricia Zandonna, Marcus and Sophia
Marcel Wolfe
Jason Wright and Family
My dear Uncle, Albert Pauchard

To my mentors:

Mr. Trevor Pereira, Mrs. Rita Alex, Mr. James Pope,
Mr. Anthony Yeow, Mr. Christopher Grieve,
Dr. Carmen Mombourquette, Mr. Robert Lussier, Ms.
Kim Carter, Mr. Doug McMillan, Dr. Yves Frenette,
Mrs. Lolita Pereira, Ms. Patricia Parisi and Mr. Glenn Domina

Special thanks to:

All of my Northmount Family, past and present
Libermann and York University Friends and Alumni
Northmount School for Boys
German International School of Toronto
Toronto Catholic District School Board
Toronto District School Board
York Region District School Board
York University
Dr. Michael Bitz and the Centre for Educational Pathways, New York
Kim Fowler and Our Kids Magazine
Lauren Carroll and Toronto4kids
Mr. Kevin A. Boyd and the Comic Book Lounge, Toronto
Mr. Joe Kilmartin, Comic Book Sage of Toronto
Mr. Doug Simpson and Paradise Comics
Mr. George Zotti and the Silver Snail
Mr. Sean Clement and the Comic Room, Scarborough
Artists Extraordinaire: Kurt Lehner, Shane
Kirschenblatt, and Marvin Law
To my heroes, Stan Lee and Neal Adams,
who I met in the summer of 2013.

Introduction

Comic books have been a lifelong pursuit of mine. I still read and collect them. This genre has opened up so many doors for me. My imagination and my teaching practice have both benefitted from exposure to these wonderful sources of literature. When I was around age twelve, a new bookshop opened in our neighbourhood. I walked by it for about two months and gave it little regard. Unlike many of the stores that could be found in downtown Toronto, this one featured nothing more than a few reference books and romance novels; neither genre captivated me, to say the least. On one grocery shopping excursion, I again strolled through the outdoor mall, when it hit me: the bookstore had placed two comic books in its front window. Now I was compelled to enter the shop. I can recall asking the owner, an elderly woman in a wheelchair, if she had any more comics than those displayed in the shop's window. Gingerly, she pointed to five large boxes and noted that each book was only a dollar. The price was right! I had also been collecting hockey cards, but the interest in those had already begun to fade, and going to the convenience store with friends to buy snacks and pop had largely replaced that former hobby, much to the chagrin of my mother, who I am sure, was seeing an increase in dental bills. The fact that I was now reading and placing whatever funds I had into a non-sugar commodity was pleasing to her. As a side note of both reflection and current observation, I find it fascinating how 1) children have so much disposable income, and 2), that although they have no gainful employment, are always in possession of some funds. My "gross domestic product" had been diverted from sugar to a serious investment in literature and imagination, the flame for which had been ignited by my cousin, William Leitmann, in 1976, when he showed me the prized possessions of his comic book collection, wrapped in plastic, and forbidden to touch. The iconic Canadian quote from John McRae's *In Flanders's Fields* and later fixture of the Montreal Canadiens' dressing room, "To you from failing hands we throw the torch, be yours to hold it high," was now passed unto me as a rite of passage for this hobby. However, for me it would be a life-long pursuit of the magic and mystery DC and Marvel Comics would wield.

It wasn't long before I had some of those long white boxes of my own, and my book depository began to grow, due to the allocation of funds for this collection from such sources as birthdays, Christmas, Easter, odd jobs, and schemes my best friend, John Hess, and I would concoct. As for school, my writing skills were not up to par, but with the careful and patient tutelage of some key teachers, and, of course, my mother, those attributes were developing nicely. A rather fascinating and parallel development occurred during those final years of elementary school. The hundreds of comic books I had collected and read were fuelling an "Age of *Enlightenment*" in terms of the ideas I was having for Social Studies, Language Arts, Science (Science Fairs), and even Mathematics. This was cross-curricular and differentiated instruction, but by my own hand, thirty years later those best practices would become a part of my teaching profession. I can recall giving a speech on comic books, which was completely improvised, and to the astonishment of the teacher, who thought I had been prolific enough to have memorized the text of my oration. At the time, some students and parents undoubtedly scoffed at the academic potential of comic books, but these perceptions were soon quieted by assessment after assessment being returned with high grades and winning Science projects. Marvel Comics' Dr. Henry Pym, or rather his alias, Ant Man, had inspired me to view Science in a totally different perspective, as did the Hulk (Dr. Bruce Banner) and DC Comics' Batman: Science was cool!

Admittedly, comic books fell in and out of favour with me during my secondary school years at Francis Libermann Catholic High School, but then seemed to have a sudden "Renaissance" in my two senior years. The Chapter, *"Comic Book Boys, Comic Book Men,"* speaks to that era. Most people who pursue this hobby would attest to a similar behavioural pattern throughout the course of their lives. The pastime resurfaced with a greater magnitude, when I began my classroom teaching career some seventeen years ago. Over two decades of classroom, international, and museum-based education the use of illustrated materials had always been part of my approach to education. The 1990's and the early 21st Century have seen the massive inclusion of multi-media and information technology into the lives of children and adults. This technological reality, driven in part by the Internet and its associative applications and devices, has permeated all aspects of life, including the classroom. A monumental paradox of great concern has arisen from the rapidity of this development, where the traditional pedagogy of the past has converged with the innovations of the future. A reconciling and hybridizing of both forces of change and stability is making waves in classrooms across Canada, the United States, and the rest of the world.

Essentially, the delivery of information, knowledge, and wisdom is under siege and conflicted. Students can now obtain data at the blink of an eye and at relatively no cost or more worrying, with little effort. I often recall the words of Jeff Goldblum's character's prophetic words in the film *Jurassic Park.*

"I'll tell you the problem with the scientific power that you're using here; it didn't require any discipline to attain it. You read what others had done and you took the next step. You didn't earn the knowledge for yourselves, so you don't take any responsibility for it. You stood on the shoulders of geniuses to accomplish something as fast as you could, and before you even knew what you had, you patented it, and packaged it, and slapped it on a plastic lunchbox."

Without sound Language Arts core skills: reading (inference, synthesis, evaluation); writing (narrative, expository, descriptive, persuasive, scaffolding process), grammar, spelling, rhetoric, vocabulary, public speaking, and debate; the technology from which we salvage information that might make us appear intelligent at a given moment, will ultimately hinder intellectual growth, creativity, and innovation. Already the decline of "the real encounter" has been compromised by virtual simulations and a darkening of Western culture that sees the experienced world as one of threat and liability. Many elementary school students and their families are faced with large classrooms, where the instruction tends to be geared to the mid-level achievers, with the struggling children attempting to gain ground, and the high performing students withering in boredom or being pressed into the service as educational assistants. Soaring attention disorder rates should come as no surprise, as the hegemony of the lighted screen supersedes the one-dimensional nature of the teacher. This situation begs the question: What innovative teaching practices can be employed to find some resolution to this 21ˢᵗ Century quandary?

Much like the paradox in Plato's <u>Republic</u>, the field of perception appears to be locked in place, thus limiting the ability of the individual to grow and see other representations of the world. Current solutions appear to advocate an approach that recognizes and teaches to the strengths and intelligences of students. This is a wonderful precept, but when dealing with the actualities of a prescribed curriculum, limited instruction time, parental support, economic and societal realities, and bureaucratic constructs, the best intentions of a well-thought-out initiative or policy become compromised. Thus, it is important that we return creative and formative agency back to our students with tangible, experience-driven activities, programs, and initiatives. These programs are bridges between the old and new pedagogies, with the reality of technology integrated with the ascendency of virtual space and time. New lessons which employ I.T., not as some prescribed tool or quick optioned outcome, but more as a fashioning tool for core skills, which cannot be circumvented by a machine or software shortcut, is the cure for apathetic reading and writing performance by students.

Returning genuine experience, performance, and organizational competencies to education will beckon a return to creativity and innovation. What we have now are pale versions of what could be. While students are becoming more self-aware of assessment, many lack the means to change their lot. The analogy of an iceberg clarifies this issue. Children see the peak of the problem, yet are doomed to repeat the crash because while they are able to view the issue, they do not have the schema to avoid a collision with their present reality. Acceptance, apathy, and resignation soon follow. Then hope succumbs to habit, and habit kills imagination, and then fate becomes reality. The reading and construction of a narrative comic book or graphic novel is but one answer.

While I do find some merit in the old axiom that suggests if students read more, they will become better writers, it is a flawed notion, because it is dependent on what children are reading, what training they have received to read and interpret text, and how imitative their capacity as writers might be. To use another analogy: I could purchase fifty airplane tickets, but after all those trips, could I fly the plane? No. The question addresses the balance between learning content and process. Giving a hungry person a fish would suffice, but according to biblical advice, teaching that person to fish would be far more charitable. Problematic to education today is that given the systematic realities of public education, teachers are transmitting a great deal of content with far less emphasis on process or performance. When I read and worked with my tome of comic books, I became rather intrigued by two tenets of the genre: 1) the development of characters, and 2) the world behind the book (author's intent, the creative process, antagonist vs. protagonist, the nature of conflict, the power of resolution, and the altering of chronological sequential story design). The comic book, in my humble opinion is the new literary turn.

As the Canadian Director of the Comic Book Project and Comics Go Global, the systemic creation of characters (physical state, emotional construction, psychological motivation, and special attributes) and the development of sequential chronological and non-chronological narratives accelerate the possibilities of increasing Language Arts competencies for students of every ability. The study and creation of comic books returns the pendulum of instruction toward an emphasis on process and on a return to creativity and innovation. It is grounded in the traditions of guided writing and mentorship and fashioned with the singular efforts of the student. While the student will be influenced by the many texts of this new literary turn, their advancement toward writing is not solely left to the axiom of osmosis. The formative process employs the power of the Internet through collaborative inputs from the global community. The summative project is posted on the Internet for the world to see.

21st Century education is at the cross-roads. It can continue to be defined by a narrow scope, benefitting the median student who can muster moments of brilliance assisted by the technology he or she so easily wields, or it can salvage what was deemed noble by tradition and merge them with the modernistic tools and educational innovations of the new century. Education has reached a point where its students and parents have either seen the limitations of the system and accepted them, or have forged some external responses to them. These retorts can be seen in the following manifestations: the rise of after-school athletics, where sports are now played that have been deemed too aggressive for school, the explosion of tutoring centres who are capitalizing on the fact that process has been a small part of the curriculum and rudimentary skills are overshadowed by what can be best described as educational pulp, and finally, the growth of the independent/private schools and home schooling, where total abdication from public systems has come to rest.

Comic books, robotics, industrial arts, instrumental music, cooking, camping, fine art, and other genuine experiential initiatives need to be examined by today's schools. The empty promises of video games and their ethereal claim to genuine experience has produced a significant student body that is resigned to mediocrity, and virtual encounters that provide neither the authentic feeling of victory, nor the reviled sting of true defeat. I have heard the claim that educators are not *"edutainers"*; this is most definitely so. However, to resign one's self to the limitations of what is currently available or achievable would be to cast one's lot in with the video gamer's notion of reality. Students are looking for the genuine, in their teachers, lessons, and activities. 21st

Century education by comic book or by hook will rest in the power of professional dynamism and the authentic teaching of practice, process, and prolonged proficiency.

Part One

—Comic Books and the New Literary Turn—

Great Scott! Comic Book Readers Are 'Smarter Than Your Average Bear'

Many young people can recall being told to put down their comic books and get serious about what they were reading.

The comic book as a form of literature has been lampooned in the media since its inception. Critiques have included the following: too simplistic, gory propaganda, sexist, morally bankrupt, and pulp fiction at best. Of course, the debate was not helped by the numerous advertisements, over the past seven decades, of novelty items such as X-ray glasses, Sea Monkeys, and muscle enhancement programs. Also the incorporation and invention of such words as "kroonk", "snikkt", and "boof" didn't help either.

However, long-time collectors and readers of these publications will argue differently. Many readers, including this one, suggested that some rather complex social, psychological, scientific, and historical themes, theories and words have been a part of these texts. The role of imagination and pictorial explanations of these aforementioned concepts abound. The institution of the Comics Code, a voluntary, self-regulating body, was created by the Comics Magazine Association of America in 1954, sought to modify and monitor the behavioural aspects of comic books as the general public complained about their content of violence, gore and horror, according to a *Time Magazine* issue on September 1954.

While vocabulary was not a major aspect of the Comics Code Criteria, it did mention as a prohibition, "Words or symbols which have acquired undesirable meanings are forbidden." The depiction and use of the words, "crime", "drugs" and "terror" were all flashpoints of censorship and debate. In 2011, the last publisher of comic books dropped the Code and all publishers favoured internal mechanisms of censorship and screening. The mere fact that the Comics Code lasted for such a duration taints the argument for this literature to take on a semblance of legitimacy. Or does it?

Comic Books and Graphic Novels Part of Curriculum

The Ontario Curriculum, for elementary education, in Language Arts, cites comic books and graphic novels as one source under the strand of Reading, in the subsection, Variety of Texts (Section 1.1) to be used in the classroom. I am certain that educators and parents alike would, upon reading this, view it as preposterous, and perhaps even label it as, "A lackluster idea from the Government of Ontario". However, this is not the case.

In a previous article, *"Will Comic Book Heroes Save Ontario's Boys?"* I suggested that, "These texts inspired students to begin reading." Eventually, once some fascinating narratives about science fiction or time travel were touched upon; students will ultimately seek out more comprehensive literature. The purpose of my current research was to go beyond the content of this literature and perform a diagnostic examination into the quality of the vocabulary (lexicon) found within these texts. Having taught both Language Arts at the elementary level (100 per cent EQAO) and at the secondary level (earlier in my career), as well as preparing students to write the independent school's Secondary School Admissions Test, the breadth of my experience facilitated the documentation of high lexicon words from 100 comic books.

The results were fascinating. Out of the 100 comic books, each issue contained an average of 825 total words of conversation and narrative text. There existed, on average, the inclusion of 27 individual, high lexicon words per title. However, numerous repetitions of these words, some even in a medium to high frequency placement level, produced some captivating conclusions. Of the 335 high lexicon words found in 100 comic books, each word was found at least twice, with 51 of those words repeating more than twice. Thus, if we subtract the higher repeating words from the total of 335 high lexicon words (284), and then multiply that number by 2 (occurrence rate), adding the cumulative occurrence rates of the 51 words, we would arrive at (568 + 422) 990 high lexicon words per 82,500 words of text (1.2 per cent).

Cumulatively, 1.2 per cent for the entire study, and an average of 3.27 per cent per issue might not seem too significant, but when the lists of catalogued words are examined, this statistic becomes impressive. This research required some comparative analysis for it to resonate. Using the qualifying 325 high lexicon words as a benchmark, the local community newspaper, *The Scarborough Mirror* had three per 825 words (0.36 per cent), the *Toronto Star* had eight per 825 words (0.96 per cent), and the *National Post* had 12 per 825 words (1.45 per cent). The average *Iron Man* comic book has 67 per 825 words (8.12 per cent). Even the researched average of 27 high lexicon words per 825 total text, denotes 3.72 per cent. Now it's impressive.

What makes these words so significant? I wanted to cross-check them against some of the words required for some significant testing moments in a student's life. Given that comic books are only one of many sources of literature being suggested under the "Variety of Texts" subsection of the Language Arts curriculum; these results are encouraging. The S.S.A.T. (Secondary School Admissions Test), administered to applicants of private/independent secondary schools in North America had a 10 per cent correlation with the list of high lexicon words. The SAT (trademark name), taken by secondary school students for university applications in the United States, had an average of 38 per cent coverage from the list. Finally the G.R.E. (Graduate Record Examination), taken by university Bachelor's Degree graduates, had an 11 per cent correlation with my research.

The Power of the Graphic Novel's Lexicon Revealed

Several conclusions can be drawn from these findings. The following may account for the aforementioned results: the education of the writers and illustrators, the broad audience (age and demographic spectrums), the perceived intelligence level of the audience, the respect the writers have for that intelligence level, and the counter-culture treatment of the audience from that of the pedantic Hollywood cinema's handling of audiences as children who require full explanations and happy endings. There was too the notion that the sophisticated, and unfairly labeled, "Comic book Geek" is on average, well-read, and to borrow a quote from the cartoons, "Smarter than your average bear." What about these results and the comic book reading world?

In April 1996, DC Comics and Marvel Comics jointly published a four-edition, limited series, which chronicled the match-ups of their greatest superheroes against each other. The story line featured one epic battle between The Hulk and Superman, with Superman winning. Five of the encounters were previously voted on by fans, and their outcomes predetermined based upon that voting. If these encounters were grounded in something other than fan voting, like the level of vocabulary that one would find in these respective publications; the final decisions in some of these bouts might be markedly different. Taking an average of five Superman titles and five Hulk titles, the Hulk has an average of 26 higher lexicon words as compared to Superman's 20. However, the 1996 result between Batman and Captain America is sustained, with Batman achieving a score of 34 higher lexicon words to Cap's 21. Perhaps, both publishing houses would consider a re-match?

Comic books are wonderful forms of entertainment and storytelling. They are the "stuff" of imagination, hope and wonder. Are they a hook to get non-readers interested in fiction? Sure. Are they a waste of a young mind's need to read compelling literature with new additions to vocabulary? They are most certainly not. Comic books are a gateway to richer literature and the exploration of new, innovative, and perhaps even, untried ideas. As much as they open a window into these intriguing aspects of the future, they also take a reader by the hand and acquaint them with powerful words from the often underused lexicon of the English language. As much as they are an excellent device for the E.S.L. (English as a Second Language) student, they also challenge the mind of the mid-level to gifted student with words, ideas, and theories that would even remain challenging for those taking a graduate school entrance examination.

You can discount this article, but do me favour, ask three friends what nucleation, pyroclastic, and rapaciousness mean? If they don't know, it might be time to give the comic book another look, or perhaps, a read.

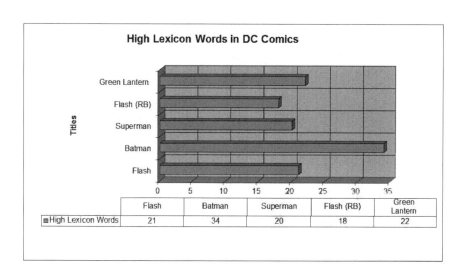

High Lexicon Words in DC Comics

	Flash	Batman	Superman	Flash (RB)	Green Lantern
High Lexicon Words	21	34	20	18	22

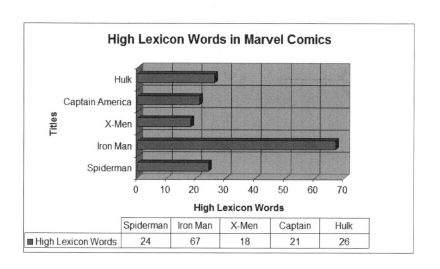

High Lexicon Words in Marvel Comics

	Spiderman	Iron Man	X-Men	Captain	Hulk
High Lexicon Words	24	67	18	21	26

Comic Book Men, Comic Book Boys: The Power of Nostalgia and the Hero

If I were to truly give credit to the formation of this article it would be to a number of people. Firstly, my cousin William, who when I was ten years old, showed me his comic collection which featured books from the later 1960's, well into the 1970's; truly some classics that he cared for a great deal. Then my friends from Francis Libermann Catholic High School, who would journey with me to Ron's Comic Room at the corner of McCowan and Lawrence each Thursday, for what was then new release day, back in the late 1980's. While the purchasing was always exciting, it was the conversations about characters, plots and what if situations that was arguably the best part of the outing. All occurring in the setting of the car of my friend Mark S. who was the holder of the largest comic book collection I had ever seen. During the 1990's, whilst in university, the hobby ebbed somewhat being replaced by the realities of raising tuition, travelling, girls, and other pursuits. However, I do recall a couple of individuals who kept the eternal flame of the graphic novel burning. The gentleman who owned Ron's Comic Room at the time, who has since sadly passed, offered this advice to me in 1995. "I know money is really tight during your university years, but all this work and struggle will pay off one day and buying a few favourite comics will return to be being a tremendous hobby, I promise you." His prognostication was true. I suppose the love of comic books is much like the regard many in North America have for baseball. To paraphrase the film Field of Dreams, America rolls on destroying, rebuilding but baseball remains a constant. Comic books have been that constant in my life, and I am sure in those adult men who still keep, revisit, and add to their collection. Through high school graduation, the university years, those graduations, my professional life, my wedding and the birth of my son Robert; all the while, there sat the comic book collection as a keeper of time and a barometer of nostalgia. Often males who carry forward a childhood or adolescent hobby into adulthood tend to be lampooned as immature or thought of as persons living in their parent's basement accomplishing nothing, and apologies in advance to Trekkers, but wearing a Star Fleet uniform. This is simply not the case.

The origin of a great deal of male creativity can be traced to some comic book collection or fantastical literature. If one were to survey a fairly sizable sample of the male population over thirty, it would come as no surprise that their desire to read and perhaps even create, innovate, and hone their individual talents may well have come from an early exposure and enthrallment with comic books. One of my best friends, Grant Zagol (who was part of the that intrepid comic book team of the 1980's) often cites the reality that all of us former Catholic school boys, who loved such titles as Superman, the X-Men, Judge Dread, and that super series Meltdown, are now all successful individuals. That former group who squeezed into my friend's hatchback now consists of engineers, managers, teachers, chemists, graphic designers and other professions; and in case readers are wondering, we did have girlfriends from time-to-time. Fascinatingly, I am sure that if you asked any of these gentlemen, their collection still exists, in some state of preservation and active gathering mode. Incidentally, most of us are still the best of friends some twenty years after high school and now and then, conversations might still begin with that immortal question, "Who do you think is stronger the Hulk, Superman, or the Thing?"

Adulthood also brings fatherhood to many. I am reminded of that eternal quote from the film Superman that has marked the time for all of us and now renders a new clarity about life, "The son becomes father, and father becomes the son." Once again, my friend Grant will argue that there are some deep seeded meanings as to why all of us (obvious Avengers reference) assemble with our respective next generation family members to collectively watch the latest offering from DC or Marvel studios together. Hopefully in the eyes of our children we hope to be heroes of sorts. Not able to leap tall buildings or ride a silver surfboard, but to be there for practices, wipe noses, dry tears, and be there to cheer. There is something else that these narratives engage in all of us, whether we are the father or the son. The notion that at one given point in time we will have to make that important heroic call, and we too, will be in the high country. Captain America is such an example of this synthesis between heroism and nostalgia, arguably the best example. His steadfast morality from generation to generation is an aspect of character development every father would seek to impart to his son. Standing up to the injustice in his world may include the courage to face a bully, and defend his peers against one. To once more quote my friend Grant, "It is the morality and strength of character we know these figures to possess that we too, want to impart to our children these examples of what was one of the factors that placed us on the right path in life." A type of character education that most schools would be hard pressed to deliver.

The characters of the comic books are mirrors for us and perhaps, reminders that as the moral fiber of society adjusts itself in directions that we may not like, it is a comfort that beyond our religious beliefs, the secular world has not quite given up on decency and the respect one's fellow citizens deserve. For our children, it is but one example that the light of hope remains in the world, and whilst we are not in possession of super powers, we can all make a difference. Of these qualities outside of heroism, remain the tenets of a virtuous person: service, fidelity, honour, loyalty, friendship, empathy, and humility. Older generations will undoubtedly be critical of their successor groups whether that be the relationship the Baby Boomers have with Generation X, or Generation X has with Gen Y, Gen Y has with the Millennials, and soon enough the Millennials with the Echoes. While time changes and the inevitable realities of aging and the alteration of society remains an aspect of reality, there is still room for nostalgia and beyond that, the very real possibility of the resurgence of these virtuous qualities. People are constantly looking for heroes and those unique moments of valour we crave to see in our fellow human beings, collectively or individually. Nostalgia is a quaint and novel state of mind, a fond remembering that generally stays trivial. Comic books could be that, but they're not. There call to action and reminders of our own capacity to do good remain a part of the living consciousness and cultural thought of present-day society. This afternoon I am off to the Comic Room, formerly Ron's Comic Room, to purchase some books that would be suitable for some of my reluctant readers. As I go down into their shop, below the Paperback Exchange, I will think for a moment of that kind gentleman who once owned the store and in due course, thank him silently for helping me to stay on the right path.

Will Comic Book Heroes
Rescue Ontario's Boys?

Think of the last time you saw an action movie with a superhero. The plot featured a crisis, but in the end justice and order were restored. Our young men in this province are in need of some rescuing of their own, and in a fascinating turn of events their champions might be those they have come to delight in on the big and small screen, but more importantly in their comic books.

The 2007-08 EQAO provincial results for Grade Six boys indicated that Reading was at 60% and Writing came in at 58% in the highest categories of Level 3 and 4 while the female numbers read 73 % and 76 % respectively. What happened? Usually an initial line from a comic book! The problem has been expressed by what Dr. Leonard Sax, an authority on gender education; identified as the feminization of education. Sax states that, "The gold standard for behaviour has become how females act in school." Sax further denotes that, "The resources for female students are far more utilized than those for males." Literature and writing have increasingly become the domain of female students because much of the popular literature and to an extent the classic works, that are presented are heavy text-based efforts with little or no visual cues or subject matter that would engage boys. Recognition of the different learning styles of males and females would be a starting point that requires teachers to shorten instruction time, address visual learners, and provide mechanisms for answering questions that are not entirely text-based. Comic books can help.

As an example, take a typical Language Arts lesson. The teacher has been speaking for longer than twenty minutes, and then asks the class to read a selection from Little House in the Woods or Romeo and Juliet for the older set. Already the boys have been given a disadvantage, can you spot it? The attention span of an elementary male student is a maximum of fifteen minutes; he is already restless and wants to get up and move. Secondly, the literature is geared to girls. It involves the nuances of relationships, communication, personal growth, and heavy pen-to-paper instruction. The average teacher will then assign questions related to plot and the development of characters and their interaction. According to subsections 1.5 and 1.6 of the Ontario Language Arts Curriculum, students are asked to make inferences based on stated (explicit) and interpreted (implicit) information in regards to these questions. The male students will provide cursory answers and in typical "results oriented fashion" arrive at the shortest and quickest possible result. Classroom literature should include themes male readers will become excited about, and there are many. Take for example James and Giant Peach, Holes, Charlie and Chocolate Factory, or even sports biographies. These are no less in quality, but are more visual, contain action and movement sequences, and speak to the world view of a young man. Questions can be answered in chart or diagram form, making use of the other aspects of the O.L.A.C. Assessing learning through the interpretation of visual media, text, dynamic language, prediction (Sec. 1.7 to 2.4), and the entire section on Media Literacy are critical to the modern world, underused by educators, and vital for male specific education. The comic book or graphic novel achieves these curricular requirements and many more in both the reading and writing strands.

Can comic book heroes rescue Ontario's boys? Unequivocally, yes! Can or should they do it alone? No. Ontario's boys need their real heroes too. Their parents and teachers need to enter into a prolonged discussion about how to facilitate boys' learning, not to restore their dominance over females, but to achieve parody. Comic books teach readers to interpret narrative through visual cues and engage imagination through prediction, anticipation, and vocabulary decoding. They are an unusual medium because they can introduce and deal with concepts that are far beyond the capacity of the reader, while promoting understanding. What cannot be found in the O.L.A.C. are the intangibles of inspiration and love of learning. Comic books open the door to these possibilities. If your son does not enjoy reading the book he has for school have him read just one chapter, but convert it to a comic strip; the same goes for writing. Aside from the aspects of comprehension and written communication, comic books by enlarge teach hope, tolerance, peace, and morality; be cautioned though, a minority are for more adult eyes and can have negative themes. Boys are looking for adventure in life and in school, if the two can be bridged by comic books then let the engineering begin.

Discovering the Big Picture: Comic Books, Writing and Conceptualization

One of the most dreaded assignments for students who are struggling with Language Arts is that initial assignment most novice teachers bestow upon their new group of students in September. They ask students to them about their summer vacation in one or more paragraph. A highly problematic venture in what many educators believe is a positive foray into a new school year. What if the summer was terrible or marred by some unfortunate happening? This is usually not the case though. Where this statement from the new teacher truly becomes terrifying for many students is the mere act of writing. There are a significant number of students who have had little preparation in the competencies required to perform any sort of writing. Writing has become an exercise in futility and frustration for many students, especially the male learner. One can view empirical evidence of this trend from the 2011-12 Ontario provincial gender statistics (EQAO, Education Quality and Accountability Office) from Grade Six students where female students are achieving 83% of the provincial standard while boys are at a lowly 67%. This should not be the case for either gender. Why are these results so unsatisfactory?

There are some time-in-memorial beliefs and correlations about writing that need to be addressed and modified for both teachers and parents. The belief that if a child is a voracious reader, they will automatically be a competent writer holds some sway, but this does not complete the hermeneutic circle for this to be a truism. While the proficient reader will show some acumen for higher levels of applicable grammar, spelling, vocabulary and perhaps even the acquisition or emulation of some the techniques their favourite authors have bequeathed them; they may not be able to fully progress beyond imitation in order to author their own work in the contexts they would wish to wield those skill sets. Reconciling their imagination into these textual connections could prove to be challenging without an inherent process to make that literal and figurative jump. The notion that a summative (final) assessment will somehow shock a young mind into action and compliance is utterly preposterous. This is a most damaging exercise for all students, but most detrimental for the male student who wishes to progress. Boys will look at a summative mark in two respects. Some may admire the mark they have achieved, remember the amount of effort required to arrive at that point, and then put forth the same exertion next time. Some of their peers who received a failing mark, will reconcile it much like they would an athletic score; better luck next time or oh well, resigning themselves to some future success. The third false principle of writing is the frustrating act of the "re-do." Our children are so socialized by the education system and its pedagogy that they have created a psychological euphoric type reaction in the act of completion, but completion without quality. Thus, asking a child to redo their writing piece is guaranteed to start a war around the homework table. How many parents have heard, "But mom, I am finished!" The same, but perhaps muted response, occurs in the class room and leads to reluctance and resentment when it comes to further performing the writing competency in school or on crucial writing assessments. So how do we solve these issues for our children?

Teaching writing is not an easy process, especially if one holds some of the aforementioned supposed truisms as some type of dogmatic gospel truth. Undoubtedly, the follower of those supposed principles will have dashed the hopes of future writers on the rocks of inflexibility and lack of vision. Recognizing writing as a process, rather than a product is a salient first step. Summative driven writing instruction at best affirms those who have some ability and freezes the potential of those who may not have any natural inclination toward the subject. The good news is that all children have fantastic imaginations and the ability to be creative. Don't scuttle that on the rocks of outdated educational practices. Initially provide a broad ranging subject that all children can identify with; for the purposes of this article, the hero. Every child has a hero: real, imagined, in the home, or in their mind. Take the students through a process of brainstorming the entire character, do this collectively! Have the students think about powerful words to describe the character's actions, reasons for doing things (motivations), personality, how that character would act in different situations, and finally their physical appearance. Congratulations, you have just done a character sketch. It is surprising that when asked to do a proper character sketch, most elementary school students will simply draw you a picture and leave it at that. The curricular component of media awareness may now be addressed. Break up the classroom structure and create groups of five students, give each of them a real emergency situation that actually occurred in the media (obviously filter out any graphic or disturbing images) and just have the students discuss what that hero, given the sum of their persona would do. Students should be talking about books they are reading, so too, should there be a significant amount of "writer talk." Now that the modeling is under way, have the students strike out on their own; independent thought scaffolded by process is powerful.

Once students have repeated the process for their own hero, have them present their results to the class. It is not unusual that the genders will view this phase differently. Keeping in mind these are not absolute truisms, but female writers often think their work is not as good as it really is, and male students often regard their work as pure gold until it is presented in the light of day. Oral presentation of this part of the paradigm is valuable in that it quenches that psychological need for the elementary school child's brain to say "Ta da! I am finished." It also equates those problematic notions of gender perception of work. Have students place that work in an identifiable folder. Do not be afraid to review basic building block functions of topic sentence construction with supporting sentences and then clearly explain how a narrative chronological structure might appear. Draw a graph if you need to. Technical infusions of skill sets in the process is critical, often educators fail their students in making assumptions about what they should know given their respective grade levels. If you are going to make an assumption, assume they don't know. Most language arts dinosaurs would now assign the summative, STOP!

What about the big picture? Students may have generated wonderful characters, empathized with them, even made the jump to the fourth dimension, where they could become the character and act accordingly to that creation's motivations, but no story exists. Without a narrative, this would be akin to putting a robust character in a theatrical production that might be presented in a food court. Students need to visualize the world behind the story and literally see it mapped out. Enter the graphic organizer. Beginning a piece of writing is easy, because everyone has some initial idea, but like a cross-country race and those who sprint at its commencement run out of gas. The graphic organizer mimics a process which should be occurring when a student is reading: the compartmentalization of salient information about all aspects of the text into to neat divisions of thought and memory that allows for contemplation and analysis, not just mere surface knowledge. Enthusiastic readers are able to do this in their active consciousness making reading enjoyable as their thought processes can ebb from the past to present and even to future predictions with the benefit of reflection and synthesis. Reluctant readers cannot perform such a task. Thus, having one's pupils construct compartmentalized graphic organizers as found in comic book panels would have the following twin effects: those students who learn to physically create these intuitive blocks of plot, character, setting, conflict, and mood and match them with a visual image can later do so without the benefit of pen and paper when reading. The inverse effect is that when reading, this component the of the writing process has the hermeneutic cascade effect of breaking down pages of written text into these same compartmentalized graphic/text units within the conscious and subconscious of the reluctant reader. What was part of an instructed process now naturally becomes intuitive for students who practice this process of writing. Guidance regarding assessment must still be a part of the student's schema of tools required by the writing process.

The last part of the process piece is the inclusion of data which informs the student how to achieve the best possible grade. Firstly, exemplars of the final product should be provided so as the student has a summative model to fashion their own work. Secondly, the teacher should provide an easy to read rubric that accounts for all facets of the writing process and the final product. In order to develop students in Language Arts, it is critical that they become assessment aware and realize exactly what components of the process and the product they are being evaluated upon. It is also imperative that each progressive level of achievement be clearly identified and distinguishable. Teachers should not jump forward to a summative assignment date unless two or three formative attempts at the culminating writing piece have been submitted for comments, editing, adjustment, and peer evaluation—not as stated earlier giving specific grades or percentages. Teachers will often ask me how this looks. The following is a step-by-step creation of a schema folder:

1. Explain the use of the writing folder, where it will be stored, and what the student will find within it.
2. Have an exercise where you and the students define, refine, and re-state the topic of the writing process.
3. Brainstorm characters, arguments, descriptions with powerful adjectives, verbs, adverbs, and nouns that are hyper-specific to the topic.
4. Find a graphic organizer that best suits the process and product of the desired outcome.
5. Review the students' graphic organizer and help them make sense of the flow and fluency of the work.
6. Review the compartmentalized meanings for each one of their panels in their graphic organizers.
7. Always review proper paragraph technique and begin some rough copies, providing only formative comments. Allow for oral presentations to peer groups or elbow partners.
8. Review exemplars, expectations, and rubrics. Be sure the students are assessment aware of what they are being evaluated upon.
9. Your schema folder is complete, assign the summative. Ultimately, the schema will evolve from a physical construct to an internalized function of the conscious and subconscious.

Writing's greatest adversary is the lack of vision, not necessarily inherent to the writer, but the lack of attention it receives from the teacher. The ability to write is changing. Students are favouring visual intelligence and spatial learning models in order to gain the necessary competencies required in Language Arts and other disciplines. While education, elementary, secondary and post-secondary, is still very much a text driven data enterprise, the ability to visualize and master text in this Information Age is vital for success. A paradigm shift which might already exist in youth culture needs to traverse the established truisms of current educational practice and perspectives and rectify itself in the manner in which literacy in reading and writing can come to ground with a need to focus on visual representations as a means of mastery through a process, not a unguided summative. Youth culture is driven by entertainment that is highly visual and arguably detrimental to the development of an analytical mind. However, should the process of creation used by modern multi-media be emulated by educators, then given rise by them to a modern process grounded in timed phases, structured by imagination, and physically compartmentalized; a new literary turn might perhaps be on the horizon. A contemporary literacy, which completes the hermeneutic relationship of the reader and the writer of all abilities, and gives rise to a student who can wield their imagination through genuine empathetic connections from outside and, while this sounds rather existential, from inside and above the text as well. The compartmentalized construction of simple comic book panels holds the key to this revolution in literacy education.

In a Fourth-Dimensional World, Boys Find a Captivating Literary Experience

Boys need action. If there were any other three words that would define the resolution of the difficulties affecting the achievement of boys on reading assessments in Ontario, I would love to know them.

As an assumption, great teachers have offered a variety of texts that are comprehensive in vocabulary, dynamic in plot, and contain a great deal of descriptions surrounding the movement and interaction of characters. They are not hamstringing (boring) them by utilizing texts that go into the grey areas of emotions, changes in communicative patterns between characters, and examinations of internal motivations that may, or may not, result in a plot change.

Fantastic language arts teachers are those whose topics must have varying content which a wide variety of boys will enjoy. Some of these include: science fiction, fantasy, historical fiction, news reports, manuals, mystery, horror and mythology. What is universal to the aforementioned headings is an intrinsic sense that they capture, captivate, hold, and enrich the literary experience of boys. If you are not there yet as educator, seriously consider that some of your choices are not resonating with your male students, and perhaps reaching into issues of engagement, classroom management and overall behaviour. If the boys aren't moving in body, then surely their mind's eye should.

Many terrific single gender and co-educational schools tout experiential learning. These are opportunities for students to supplement the textbook and the desk, and offer a chance to use their hands in order to gain a greater understanding of what is being taught. Science does this with experiments, social studies with museums, mathematics with manipulatives and computer graphic modules, and language arts with drama.

Is there something beyond drama that could close the connection of meaning for students, especially male students? This is not to discount drama; it is a valuable tool for learning. However, it has its limitations. Most teachers will use text that is already in a scripted format, having the students read, and then possibly act out a scene. Improvisational theatre, although more creative, is limited by the desire of the students to work through a scene and the much needed free flow of imagination. It can be difficult to keep to a story line or central theme.

Is there another approach? Might it be possible for the students to become the characters they are reading? Could they assume the character's traits, allowing for interpretation and action to occur based on those character compositions and the artificial realities created by the text, in terms of setting, theme, characters, plot and mood?

Guided Through Character Sketching

In short, the answer is," yes." The process begins with the examination of a character that previously existed within the text, or a character that could be derived from the "world of the text." We can call this process a character sketch. Oddly enough, many students will tell you that a character sketch is the drawing of a character. While that might be a part of the process, it is by no means the entire exercise. Students from the first grade onward can be guided through a process of character sketching. The following categories can be added to the paradigm as the student progresses further in elementary school:

physical description, feelings, motivations, reactions, relationships (to other characters), goals, desires and origins.

The creation of this character biography will take the child so far into the text, which ideas regarding meaning can vault over mere knowledge to the more critical tenets of analysis and synthesis. When students have the ability to surpass understanding they can grasp, they seize factors that reflect a higher intelligence level. Reading then becomes multi-dimensional. Students can begin to predict, run various scenarios, and develop alternate endings.

According to educational theory, "There has been an ongoing challenge to 20th-century learning which was largely a mechanical cause-and-effect formula to what should exist now: a complex model of learning that contains complex unities, which are spontaneous, unpredictable, irreducible, contextual, and vibrantly sufficient; in brief, they are adaptive," according to *Engaging Minds: Learning and Teaching in a Complex World* by Brent Davis, Dennis Sumara and Rebecca Luce-Davis. In order to make this leap, students must be given the correct schema, so that connections to text can go beyond simple associative memory linking. While connections to text can be found by comparative personal experience with another text, a personal experience, or some encounter with traditional or new media, a more genuine correlation might be found when the aforementioned Complex Model of Learning is engaged. Thus, "through deliberate engagements of the imagination, one's sphere of experience might be expanded, opening the door to new perceptual and interpretative possibilities," according to *Engaging Minds*.

A Virtual World for Character Discovery and Interpretation

If a teacher of literacy were to go through the lesson of the comprehensive character sketch, and then do the same analysis of the setting, a virtual world for character discovery and interpretation might be made possible. Although all fictional text requires some suspension of belief, a schematic of a four-dimensional world might be able to be constructed by the teacher and students in concert with each other. Going beyond the physical aspects of a simple setting are the following factors one must include when fashioning this new world of chaotic perceptual meaning: assumptions, technology, boundaries, beliefs, laws of physics, jurisprudence, science, time, nature and technology.

Just as much as the characters are made to be dynamic, so too must the world from which students will draw interpretation. What draws the students' enthusiasm is that their character that is placed into this world is not a casual observer or actor, their mere presence and activity initiates the creation of expanding and contracting hermeneutic circles of meaning for the individual pupil, the collective and subsequent modifications to the original text's narrative. This narrative has undergone the transition from the one-dimensional vision of its author to the complex sphere of the student-teacher collective where the base underpinnings of meaning dictate the boundaries of the new dimension, not necessarily the canon of the book. Successful interpretation and interaction will be graded by adherence to the parameters, assumptions and codes of the book.

It is at this point where the teacher must supersede the author and to a degree assume his or her voice. The educator must develop mechanisms to facilitate the three types of conflict found in most non-fiction texts. These conflicts now become interactive and can cost the student/character penalties in regards to engagement and physical conflict with the newly constructed environment. Characters will live, fight, earn treasure, be wounded, and possibly perish. The decisions are in the hands of the student, but crafted by the canon of the text and the constructed character's profile. This ushers in a new dimension of experiencing a book. While this role-playing reality lends itself best to fantasy, science fiction and history, it can be crafted to suit most literature genres. All teachers want the book to come alive and take our students by the hand, but sometimes this process must be facilitated by the educator.

For Grade 5 Students, Fiction Meets Non-Fiction

As cross-curricular activities, my Grade 5 students at Northmount School designed a mathematical grid, developed a scale of size, geographic legend and directions. They then used their notes from the novel we were reading to define the realities of the spatial environment their characters would have to react to. Two boys constructed a store and charged sales tax, a concept we covered in mathematics. Others designed geographical features true to the canon of the book, and foundational in science and social studies texts. Fiction met non-fiction. As a collective we assigned each character powers and negotiated how losses would be handled with the roll of a dice and the subtraction of points.

For the keen observer, this seems to be a lot like other role-playing games. The lesson plan is far more complex and cerebral. Those games have worlds created and characters defined. While there is some creativity in the nuance of the characters and even the capacity to create one's own maps, the creative and interpretive control and negotiation of perception, meaning, and novel canon do not exist.

The fourth-dimensional world is the hermeneutic creation of multiple meanings, which come from the text, but pass through the competencies and mindset of the students. The novel comes alive, but the students take each other by the hand and create a whole new schema of understanding and connection fuelled by their actions and experiences in a world they have fashioned. Scenarios play out with the higher capacity thinking skills of analysis, synthesis, prediction and evaluation. Boys' literacy must be this engaging, so that all levels of ability within the classroom are privy to insights and thinking that has direct consequences on live play. Surmising grey areas and implicit content become the purview of the player, and extends far beyond the prowess of the reader.

Four-dimensional literacy and engagement will offer boys the chance to go further into a text than what was thought to be possible. If the possibilities are redefined, and if it is the student who is doing it, learning will ebb and flow from the text through the mind, to the game, and through time.

Ten Reasons Why Children Should Read Comic Books

Sadly, comic books have often been looked at as a second-rate form of literature. Educators and parents, alike, have long preferred books that were heavy on text, and light on illustrations. Proclaiming "the classics" as a means by which all children should be educated was forever at the foundation of Language Arts instruction. A new generation of teachers are rediscovering the immense value of these texts. While not all comic books are suited for children and teens, and some are written for adults, by adults; the truth remains: they are a powerful and useful genre for the development of a student's capacity to comprehend and analyze literature, while dramatically improving their proficiency in Language Arts.

Their Lexicon of Complex Words is higher than Most Publications

In a personal and published study of over 1,000 comics and their inclusion of higher order words, most comic books and graphic novels featured an astonishing 36%-76% of their text as representative of language found in senior secondary school and college/university placement tests. Most other periodicals and newspapers only garnered 14% of these higher lexicon words.

Improvement of Memory Skills

With the world becoming very media/visually literate, someone who is learning English or a reluctant reader/writer could use the comic book as a means of engaging a sense of prediction and revision at the same time, by following sequential design, yet being able to visually flip back and restore the immediate visual hit again and again. This **informed memory access** (I.M.A.) and renewal is central to learning English in its colloquial and contextual element.

Introduction to non-linear storytelling

Many comic book writers tend to construct story arcs, over long periods of time. This requires readers to serialize their approach and wait a few weeks for the next installment. Charles Dickens did the same with his work. This affords the reader some time to contemplate the story. Even though the text might be presented in a chronological and sequential text-to-image presentation, the story arc can jump from past to present, and to future, all in the same narrative.

Multiple Gateways to Higher Order Literacy

Comic books serve reluctant readers best as an initial gateway to reading. They are the hook by which children have come to appreciate literacy. In a January 2013 interview, Silver Snail owner, George Zotti spoke about the new literary turn which encompasses all of the building blocks of media literacy, which, at its core, remains the written word. When asked about the literacy of the comic book, Zotti noted, "They are the gateway to books, the ability to bequeath the gift of wanting to read and continuing to do so is a tremendous present; comics are just as good as any novel." Comic books provide further gateways up the literacy continuum with graphic novels like *Kill Shakespeare* that introduce more complex competencies like character amalgamation, prediction, and analysis.

Lessons in Character Sketches and Character Development

Attempt the following experiment with any elementary or middle school student: have the student produce a character sketch. Most students will actually produce a drawing. Comic books provide multiple examples of how characters are structured, based on a back story, motivations, reaction to setting and place, and movement through plots as minor and major characters, and the introduction of what it means to be an antagonist and protagonist, and why this has developed. They offer a blueprint for the identification and replication of advanced writing techniques.

Reluctant Readers can Picture Plot Points

If a reluctant reader cannot picture specific plot points they will most likely become lost and set the book down. The ability to follow and then comment upon plot is central to the development of childhood literacy. Children who are struggling with reading can easily *discover the world behind the book*, as their more proficient peers do, but can do so with the assistance of a comic book or graphic novel. Shakespeare is the quintessential example.

Rekindle the Imagination and a Desire to Write

George Bernard Shaw once said, ""Imitation is not just the sincerest form of flattery—it's the sincerest form of learning." The sheer exposure to the imagination of the comic book writers and artists is a virtual guarantee that some of what children have read will adhere to them. One of the most significant connections a student can make is a *text-to-self* construction. Even if imitative, this is the spark that will fuel a love of reading and writing.

Allows the Framing of New Literary Worlds by Readers

Using the canon of the comic book story, students can explore the world and nature of the characters they have been reading about and utilize such higher end Language Arts skills such as meta-cognition, prediction, and synthesis to write continuations.

The Expansion of Imagination

Children now live in a world framed too much by boundaries, rules, and for that matter, the limited imagination of others. Comic books, although fashioned in the "literary world" of its creators, have a unique quality that anything can happen. Unpredictability and magic still exist. Due to the twin realities of monthly publication and the time invested in reading, the imagination of the reader can expand in incalculable directions.

Improve Student Grades and EQAO/CAT Scores

Parents might be surprised to learn that the Ontario EQAO and the CAT4 (Canadian Achievement Test) both feature comic strips and sequential narratives in their assessment of reading and writing. All of the tenets of Language Arts: plot, character, conflict, mood, setting, and even vocabulary can be bolstered by the reading and creation of comic books. Male readers would especially be aided by their continued exposure to this genre.

The aforementioned ten reasons might motivate you to re-examine your view on comic books. Lastly, and perhaps the most salient point regarding the genre: students will self-select what they wish to read. The revival of comic books can be married to the inclusion of a variety of texts that go below and beyond a reader's current ability. Comic books and graphic novels are gateways to success in literacy, at any level of ability.

A Comic Book Era:
What Are Appropriate Comic
Books for Certain Ages?

Comic books are experiencing a post-golden age with the Internet and Hollywood movies garnering record profits for publishing houses that have either licensed their iconic characters to them, or have been incorporating them, as a whole, into their multinational business embrace. To quote a certain friendly neighborhood web slinger, "With great power comes great responsibility." To a large extent, this mantle of social responsibility has been exercised quite diligently by such mainstays as DC and Marvel Comics. As a keen observer of digital media and film, there is a genuine effort to include the younger set in the echo of these major productions, like Batman and the Avengers. The adjustment comes in the form of animated features that pardon the pun, take the punch out of their silver screen versions. Saturday morning cartoons are such examples, but be warned though, there are animated versions of our heroes that are still not for the under 16-crowd. If double entendre and innuendo are not acceptable, these long-form animated films should be avoided. However, what about comic books and their rating systems?

The history of the Comics Code, a self-censoring apparatus of the industry, which lasted from 1954 to January 2011, was created, in part, to censor comic books of inappropriate material, initially for horror comics, and then to adult themes and depictions of criminality that crept into the genre. Parents take note, Marvel created a publishing division for the 18+ crowd, called Epic Comics, with DC doing the same with Vertigo. In 2001, Marvel introduced its own rating system, with DC abandoning the Comics Code in 2011, for a similar initiative to that of Marvel Comics. Initially, the Comics Code worked because many retailers would ultimately refuse to sell any publications without the printed sanction of the Comics Code. This changed when new mediums of retail emerged, such as the specialty comic book store, direct mail initiatives, and the proliferation of comics to all sorts of retail concerns. Adding the proverbial nail in the coffin was the lack of enforcement of the Code. **There also exists a rather fascinating paradox to the comic book/graphic novel genre. From their inception, these books were designed with the pre-adolescent to adolescent person in mind. What has evolved over several decades is a semi-stationary audience that has grown up with these characters, creating a hermeneutic circle that drives the tolerance and acceptance of certain themes beyond the genesis of its original audience and intent.** So then, where does this leave the conscientious parent?

As a teacher and parent, a favourite website has been <u>www.screenit.</u> <u>com</u> and for some book reviews (<u>www.commonsensemedia.org</u>). Keeping in mind, a ratings system works on generalities and spectrums of tolerance and acceptance; thus, even with the most comprehensive editing and vetting systems, in the end, it comes down to the subjectivity and involvement of the supervising parent. What I enjoy about the aforementioned websites is that aside from taking on the "biggies" nudity, violence, coarse language, and mature themes, they also address the following parental concerns: smoking, drug use, disrespect, blasphemy, rude conduct, and other morally unacceptable traits. If only the rating of comics could do that! They cannot, that interpretation of the spectrum is up to the negotiation of the parent with the medium. Keeping those predications in mind, I have found some comic books that are indeed suitable for children.

Image Comics' *Super Dinosaur*: Stocked with massive action, a strong vocabulary and plot that is both fascinating and attractive to children that are into robotics, cyborgs, and dinosaurs. To quote one of its fans, from its reader response section: "We need more all-ages comics. There is a drive to make them more adult themed, but these stories are timeless."

Marvel Comics' *Marvel Universe Ultimate Spider-Man*: Rated All Ages, this version of Spider-Man is much like the animated series that is produced for the YTV and Nickelodeon audiences. It features all the mainstay characters, but without the gratuitous violence and innuendo. The story is still quite punchy and carries the reader.

DC Comics' *Batman Li'L Gotham*: is rated under the DC system as "E for Everyone", (Much like a video game rating). I found this comic to be a little unusual, as I know how these characters operate in an older milieu and couldn't help be pensive as I turned the pages. However, the book is reimagined with the well-known Gotham heroes, and villains are fashioned as kids. It's a neat read, but children might find it too text heavy and the animation a bit jumbled.

Kaboom Comics' *Adventure Time*: This is an enjoyable read and would be great for students from Grade 4 to 6. The characters are witty, and while there is some disrespectful language, there is no profanity and a fairly engaging plot. I even learned something about Information Technology in issue #13. Kaboom offers some other great titles, refreshing some classics like Garfield and Peanuts, and introducing new characters like *Hero Bear and the Kid*, which is quite entertaining.

Bongo Comics' *Futurama* and the *Simpsons* are Matt Groening's television series on the pages of a comic book. This one is one of those spectrums of subjectivity decisions. If you permit your children to watch these television shows, the content of the books is fairly close to that of the other media. Not every child will appreciate or understand the cultural references, sarcasm, and social critique. The readership is perhaps more suitable for a teenager.

Archaia Entertainment's *Mouse Guard Labyrinth and other Stories* is a fascinating read with many short animated stories revolving around morality and virtue. Some of the vocabulary is quite advanced, but the depictions of plot and character are quite astounding. My favorite of the vignettes was the classically illustrated, *The Tale of Baldwin the Brave*, which ends with the slightly altered and iconic phrase by Edmund Burke, "Evil will prevail if good mice do nothing."

Scholastic's *Bone* by Jeff Smith is an engaging book for boys, but yet again, I must predicate the recommendation on the spectrum of subjectivity and allowance of certain themes. *Bone* has been deemed inappropriate by some parents for the inclusion of smoking and drinking, and the level of violence within its pages. In 2010, a Missouri woman lobbied to have the books removed from the school library for her perception of sexual tension between the characters. On the other end of the permissible spectrum, the book's plot moves quickly and the story arch truly captures the attention of the reader. Literacy commentators likened the themes in *Bone* to similar ones found in literature for the same elementary group, often comparing it to a hybrid *Lord of the Rings* and some early Disney work. Rated one of the best graphic novels of all time, it is worth taking a look at. It was also named one of the top graphic novels by *Time Magazine*.

Another book for the eight to ten year old crowd is by Kazu Kibuishi's *Amulet*. Grounded in the fantasy genre, the plot truly holds the reader and presents exciting moments with monsters, vampires, robots, and ghosts. There are some potentially troubling moments with the death of a parent and the characters (children) who seem to be in constant peril. However, its one-hundred and eighty-five page narrative is truly dynamic, but somewhat light on text.

Kevin Boyd, owner of Toronto's *Comic Book Lounge and Gallery* suggested that the *Bone* and *Amulet* would be ideal for the student who is between the ages of ten and fifteen. When asked about the appropriate age to transfer to the comics that mainstream adults and older adolescents read, he put forth the range of the much older teenager and young adult. His other recommendations for younger teens and pre-teens included *The Road to Oz* and the *Emerald City* series.

Louis Riel, A Comic-Strip Biography, by Chester Brown is a triumph of writing in the comic book genre. It is incredibly thorough, providing an account of the life and tribulations of Louis Riel and a back story grounded in Canadian History and Geography that most non-fiction textbooks would only hope to feature. The detailed maps and endnotes alone are worth reading this graphic novel. Understanding the plight of the First Nations and Metis during the tumultuous events of the mid to late 19th Century in Manitoba and the West come to life in Brown's account through the protracted conflict Riel has with the federal Government. While Brown admits to openly leaving large aspects of Riel's life out of his account, **he taps into a unique quality many graphic novels and comic books offer: "In case this book triggers a desire to read further . . ."**

Two Generals by Scott Chantler was reviewed for me by **eminent Canadian war historian, Dr. Eric McGeer** (He is a member of Northmount School's faculty). Some thoughts on *Two Generals*. By strange coincidence, I knew Lieutenant Chantler and some of the people mentioned in this book. I was thinking of writing a book about the battle in which they were at a town called Buron, and I interviewed a number of the veterans who had taken part. Chantler was in his early eighties, still sharp as a tack, and my notes concur with the description in the book. So, full marks for accurate depiction of his recollections.

On closer second reading, I think that the book would be well suited to Grade 6 or older. The narrative line is not straight, requiring the young reader to understand the use of flashbacks or other transpositions in the story, and this might cause confusion to younger readers who are used to a sequential narrative. There are some troubling scenes (accidents, battle situations, murder of prisoners of war) that might distress younger readers, and would need some explanation if presented to Grade 6 and older. But on the whole, the story the book tells is valuable to mature readers. It introduces them to the history of Canada's involvement in the Second World War, and it tells the story through the reminiscences of a historical participant in the events described, which would lead young readers to consider the question of sources, memory, subjectivity and objectivity, and historical context. The book could provide a starting point for a wider discussion of how history is recorded and how versatile a perspective this kind of illustrated narrative provides.

What is the appropriate age for comic books and graphic novels? Ultimately, that is the decision of two parties that should always be in close communication with each other: the parents and teachers. While reviewers, authors, and publishers can recommend age limits, they should always be taken with a grain of salt and, primarily, with the standards of the family in mind. Much like vetting Halloween candy or films, this genre should be approached in the same fashion. The intent of this article was to quash the idea of absolute limitations and censorship, in favour of an informed and involved educational and parental tandem of authority. The exclusion of reading material for children can be very easy by avoiding publishers who clearly market to an adult audience and mainstream DC and Marvel titles that should be read only by teenagers in their senior years and by young adults. Conversely, inclusion can also be of little debate when children are reading classic literature that has been animated for them. Where the advisory becomes more subjective is with books that are denoted for your child's age range, but might feature aspects of the popular culture you find objectionable in certain frequencies of appearance or delivery based on your family's standards. This subjective spectrum of acceptable and tolerable themes, images, and messages comes down to the discerning and interventionist eyes of the parent and teacher. There is no question that the graphic novel and the comic book can aid both the reluctant and proficient Language Arts student with scaffolding, writing, reading comprehension, growth of vocabulary, sequential and non-sequential thought processes, planning, synthesis and evaluation at different points of development from the gateway of introduction to literature and then on to higher points of competency development. As an analogous comparison to the Internet, there exists tremendous power to educate, but that comes with awesome responsibility to wield the resource correctly.

Off the Pages of Wonder and into the Classroom:
Comic Books Come to the Rescue

Have you ever felt as if you were hanging by a thread? Had that sinking feeling where your feet were going deeper into quicksand? Had knots in your stomach as if a super villain were chasing you? Many students who are both, struggling and doing well in reading and writing, experience those feelings. They report feeling frozen, as if being struck by a freeze ray or tractor beam. While a galactic empire or rogue may not be responsible, your favourite superhero could actually rescue you from these emotions of dread and fearfulness, regarding Language Arts! How is this possible?

A good many parents look at comic books as a simple form of literature, not to be taken seriously. However, just like a sudden gust of wind, or a flash of light, or even a streak in the sky, comic books deserve a second look or double take. Did you know that when compared to the word lists of tests, which older students take to get into some secondary schools and university programs, comic book words from a sample of over 1,000 comic books showed up 45%-60% of the time on these challenging assessments? In comparison, your local and national newspapers had these complex words appear only 5%-20% on the same tests. Adults who had read comic books all of their lives look back to their teenage years and can recall that the ideas in these graphic novels opened gateway, after gateway to new ideas in Science, Technology, History, Geography, Mathematics and, of course, Language Arts. One of Toronto's most exciting stops on the comic book trail, the Silver Snail, has an owner who said exactly that. George Zotti stated, "All of the words in Marvel's *Iron Man* comic book inspired me to find out more meanings about the terms the author used." So the words of our heroes have loosened the bonds of the twin villains known as "Mr. Repetition" and "Captain Simplicity."

"I found I had to choose my words carefully and plan ahead with an organizer when I was writing." **Tyler T., 9 (Grade 4)**

One of the most fearful situations in reading and writing is when boys and girls come across the entity known as "The Void." This invisible adversary introduces itself at the point when the teacher utters the words that bring him to life. "Please write a few paragraphs on a story where you discover something." Enter "The Void!" He can paralyze with one grasp of a pencil and can force you to say your oath of allegiance to him, "I don't know where to start." Fear not, the comic book and its heroes are here to save you. Written in sequential and chronological form, the comic book structure offers an immediate model to which you can fashion a story. It is more than just beginning, middle, and end. That you know, and that is not enough to defeat "The Void." The structure of the graphic novel shows you how to write good descriptive passages that follow different story lines that mould into one. That technique is difficult to teach, but when modelled in a comic book, it comes to life!

THE COMIC BOOK PROJECT
COMIC BOOK CANVAS

Name: _Nikolas H._   Program/School: _Northmount_   Grade: _5_

Playing with time and how to write narratives that make the reader hooked to your story are key. The blocking and spacing of stories in comic books offers a unique step-by-step model for composition.

"I avoided "The Void" because I knew that I just couldn't start writing; instead, I used graphic organizers as a stepping stone to finishing my work. My spelling and grammar became better because I edited the mistakes ahead of time." **Mark D. 8 (Grade 4)**

An excellent story idea might have come to mind, but having no one to act in it would be a real shame. Your story with all of its twists and turns, hidden meanings, surprises, and high adventure would be like an empty stage without actors. Many comic books take some serious time in developing their characters. They fashion a personal history for them and an origin story, answering the big questions surrounding the character's powers and past. You, too, can do more than just draw your character. Think about the comic book model and create points for these four categories: physical appearance, emotions, motivations, and personality traits. You might think that this will take a long time, but in reality if you do all the planning based on the modelling, set out by such storied companies as DC and Marvel, you will not only find writing will go faster, but it will be so much more enjoyable. With joy comes passion, and with passion, high marks!

"We know how to speak in conversations, but writing them was challenging. We had to know how two characters we invented actually spoke to each other." **Peter D., 12 (Grade 6)**

"I enjoyed this writing because we made up our own worlds with their own rules and had to make our characters fit." **Ryan L., 12 (Grade 6)**

"Keeping the reader's attention also kept my enthusiasm for writing; I wanted to write exciting scenes for myself and also for my readers!" **Mark D., 8 (Grade 4)**

"Writing my own comics helped me bring character that I always had in my mind to life on paper." **David D, 9 (Grade 5)**

"Designing and studying comics triggered my imagination and helped me to clearly write stories." **Ian V., 10 (Grade 5)**

All of you have deep imaginations like a cavern in a mysterious mountain. Comic books and graphic novels, their comprehension and design (by professional or by student), can provide you with tools like a flash light, a ring of invisibility, and a treasure map to reach into those places where your dreams exist, and launch them on to paper. They can rescue you from Level 2 or C, and blast you off into the world of creativity and enjoyable writing. Whether it comes from a caped crusader or your friendly neighbourhood web-slinger, reach out and grab the hand of a comic hero and their stories, you might find some special powers of your own!

Toronto's Comic Book Empire Writes Back:
A Preface to Culture and Literacy

Whether it was D.C. Comics' <u>Secret Origins</u> (1961, 1973-74, 1986-90)[1] or the thorough anthology of Marvel Comics, entitled <u>The Marvel Universe</u> (1989-90),[2] the desire to learn the back story of the dynamic and larger-than-life characters these works fostered in so many young minds, and with so many generations, made these books very popular. There exists a parallel fascination and element to the culture of the graphic novel and comic book, which many have not chosen to include as part of their research, or if they have, it has been addressed as trivial at worst, and at best, a tertiary component of their construction of the paradigm surrounding these hybrids of art and narrative. Most scholarship focuses upon the reader, the content of the text, and the circumstances and development of its creators, in a trinity of meaning. However, there is a fourth dimension that perhaps has been forgotten. It is the experience and observation of purchasing comics and the environments that foster and maintain a fluid community of memory amongst their patrons, which demands an inclusion into the understanding of the genre of comic books and their popularity. The remarkable insights of the stalwarts of these specialized books and unique literacies offer a new dimension to the understanding of a medium that features harmonized text with spectacular illustrative power. As much as their knowledge frames a new understanding for the student of the comic book era, so, too, does their collective framing of an environment, a "scene", and most importantly a community, to make it a total encounter for the mind, the body, and soul of those who are growing up, have grown up, and who live by the mantra, "Geek is sheik."

The Comic Book Lounge and Gallery (587A College St.) is, by its owners' words, "a store and a community space"[3]. However, that's really not quite it by a long shot. The business acumen of its owner Kevin A. Boyd, coupled with the store's secret weapon and its manager, Mr. Joe Kilmartin, whose gregarious nature, affable and kind personality, and above all, thorough knowledge of all things comic and cultural, adds a unique dimension to the climate of literacy, which exists there. If the experience of reading and collecting transcends the two-dimensional world of the animated page into a live human exchange of ideas, friendship, and mutual appreciation of talents, then that physical space of the literary world fuels not only its existence, but its long-term success. Insights into the success of this form of literacy provide a dual evolution of the importance of a retail space and the uniqueness of its product. Kilmartin posits, "Comic books are more than a genre, they are in fact a type of universal medium which can be applied to other contexts besides the familiar graphic novel."[4] This wide appeal and conscious understanding of the text features and arrangements transcend what many people would believe is their natural audience: young males between the ages of 10 to 30, and in excess of that range. An understanding of the client base and what he demands and perceives from his retail experience are everything to the financial viability of a store like The Comic Book Lounge and Gallery. It has under its ownership, management, and core community defined its literary environment. One clearly ascertains that there is a community of persons who are participatory through media literacy, a highly literate mindset, and media awareness that act as foil and mirror for the professionals of the comic book industry in Toronto. There is a genuine symbiosis between the fan, the reader, the creator, and the visual artist, taking place on the literal, virtual, and physical plane of what can be defined as community in this digital age.

Examining the need for community, literacy, and belonging to this hybrid space of physical and virtual pop culture rests a question regarding its future: Toronto's cultural mosaic continues to expand how the world of comic book works and how its peripheral environments might adjust. Kilmartin ingeniously ties the thread together with the following:

"There exists an ebb and flow to the medium that perhaps can be marked by time. 19th Century English literature had been serialized in story arcs, like the works of Charles Dickens. Globally, comic books arose out of the same source material as political cartoons, yet North American literature rested on the escapades of the super hero in a soap opera or Disney comedic operetta, while those of Europe and Asia were grounded in long-form text and had an adventure/mystery tone. Early to mid-Twentieth Century comparisons cite the North American comic book directed to adolescent audience, while those in Europe favoured an adult readership."[5]

Fascinatingly, the rise of the comic book retail environment seemed to coincide with a *new literary and demographic turn*. This reconstituted revolution evolved the comic book from its place in the local convenience store to a more specially defined retail space, attracting its dedicated base, as well as a more discerning and informed reader and collector. The industry would experience a strange schism of sorts when the comic book had been reduced to a twenty-two page collector's card, devoid of much literacy and heavy on illustrations. Joe Kilmartin continued, "The 1990's were in some ways a restoration of an industry devoid of much literacy and heavy on illustrations.

Marvel and DC brought in British writers to turn the tide during this decade. The writers who come to mind are Grant Morrison (although he had been there a while already at that point) Warren Ellis, Garth Ennis, and John Wagner, to name a few."[6] Out of the dark 1990's ascended a more balanced periodical with fascinating (positive) stories matched with the artwork of a new generation. So, too, did the further attraction of persons who were new to the country of comic books. When asked about this phenomenon, Kilmartin had a fascinating observation, "With the world becoming very media/visually literate, someone who is learning English could use the comic book engaging a sense of prediction and revision at the same time, by following sequential design, yet being able to visually flip back and restore the immediate visual hit again and again."[7] This **informed memory access** (I.M.A.) and renewal is at the heart of the means to learn English in its colloquial and contextual element, while discerning the culture from which it had been derived in a parallel process to the native English speaker, defining the world of the comic book, which for the ESL/ELL learner includes the new world of his country. Much was learned that day at the foot of the master. An understanding of this literacy in historical and modern construct fosters a further segment to the Comic Book Lounge and Gallery's pool of clients; the nostalgia of the familiar and reintroduction of popular culture to the next generation is the other.

Aside from events grounded in the calendar year (Fan Expo, Comic Con etc.), every emerging and successful literary culture needs an epicentre, a cathedral of sorts. Just as the religious buildings of the past millennium have inspired the faithful, so too, does the mere mention of the name: *The Silver Snail*. Being a kid from suburbia in the 1980's, my friends and I did have our beloved local comic store, *Ron's Comic*

Room, which out of respect, loyalty, and nostalgia we still frequent. However, it was serious business when we made the trek downtown to go to *The Silver Snail*. As I sat down with one of the owners, George Zotti (who, with all due respect, looks like a combination of Francis Ford Coppola or George Lucas—it doesn't help that there is a life-size R2D2 at The Snail) defined the atmosphere perfectly through his own experience. "Nothing like it existed in my mind, it (Silver Snail) was tailor made for a boy who was nine; it was a utopia for boys."[8] He continued, "Visitors are assaulted by colour, and the overwhelming smell of the printed paper."[9] He's right. The boy inside this forty-two year-old father and vice-principal quickly came out as I ascended the stairs of *The Silver Snail*'s new location on a second floor building north of Yonge and Dundas and saw a life-size, hanging Spider-man! With a gaping mouth, all I could muster was WOW! Zotti called *The Silver Snail*, "a destination shop."[10] "People come from all over to visit us."[11] He, too, will talk of the new literary turn which encompasses all of the building blocks of media literacy, which at its core remains the written word. When asked about the literacy of the comic book, Zotti posits, "They are the gateway to books, the ability to bequeath the gift of wanting to read and continuing to do so is a tremendous present; comics are just as good as any novel."[12] If that gateway is

decorated with life-size heroes, an R2D2, and a hanging Spider Man, which in turn, stokes the power of that gift, then this is the inspirational environment from which it has its origin.

Much can be noted about the power of the lexicon found in comic books. Zotti harkened back to his youth and related an account of how Iron Man had led him to the dictionary. I found this observation to be remarkably fascinating as *Iron Man* was one of the highest rated comic books in a 2012 study I conducted on high frequency and high lexicon words in over one thousand comic books per title. Mr. Zotti stated, "When I was in Grade 5 or 6, I read a lot of *Iron Man*. He was identified as the Chairman of the Avengers. I didn't know what the word 'Chairman' meant and like many other words in *Iron Man*, I needed to know. So I went to the dictionary. From looking up words to become a better reader, George Zotti cited that process."[13] He continued, "The ability to read is often linked to the ability to remember; while you can retain better aspects from a tablet, the instant gratification of that memory function does affect deficiencies in memory, spelling, and contextual meaning. The framing of these competencies is subverted by the technology of the tablet."[14] While digital comics might be a part of the future, the nostalgia and resonance of the print editions remain virtually sacrosanct with readers and collectors alike. Zotti cited the example of a woman from India who purchases stacks of Batman for her brother in India.[15] He suggests that the genre's ability to couple a narrative within a journey and then create a parallel journey for the reader drives the genre forward.[16] While he may cite the resurrection of the record store and its vinyl product being akin to the survival and success of the comic book store, his business model has one unique advantage. Nostalgia is created at a break-neck speed, as the peripherals to the literacy break through the bonds of time and has extraordinary relevance in the past, present and future. The timelessness of the characters and their narratives are reinvented with every generation sparking fandom in the present and a gold mine of discovery for the past.

Travelling uptown, north of Yonge and Lawrence resides *Paradise Comics*. It specializes in the classics. A treasure trove of Gold, Silver, and Bronze Age Comic Books (modern up-to-date, titles too), as well as a fabulous selection of graphic novels await the visitor. Sometimes people might be hesitant to enter comic book stores if they are new to collecting. The welcoming nature of Doug Simpson and his staff put all those concerns to rest. The approach here seems to be tailored to the level of experience of the customer. Simpson credits the success of his store, in terms of increasing literacy, to the specialities of the store being for both older and younger readers, and the atmosphere that fosters this literacy. "The strength of our store is predicated on the variety of product, the knowledge we have of the titles, and the added feature of discerning the appropriateness of books for children."[17]

Our intrepid Northmount Comic Book Club first ventured into *Paradise Comics* some three years ago where Simpson and his staff were extremely knowledgeable, and most impressively pointed out selections that boys would enjoy reading, and those they should place back on the shelves because of some content not fit for young readers. This was terrific especially for someone in education who is attempting to hook students into reading some of the fine literature that can be found in comic books and graphic novels.

Simpson's take on the attractiveness of literacy in comic books comes from an understanding of the draw of what he called the *Stan Lee method of Six Panel Story Production*. He postulated that, "Readers enjoyed the familiarity of the six panel approach because of their conduciveness to the language arts skill sets of Prediction and Identification through Empathy."[18] These two factors have allowed literature to become extremely accessible and, in the language of the special needs educator, "chunked" for cohesive and short comprehension. Simpson has a unique feel for this reverse engineering of literature. He recognizes an inherent barrier appears to exist for those readers less adept to reading heavy text treatments, who might avoid their introduction or acquisition for decades, were it not for the transference of novels and long-form stories into the "Stan Lee Method". Simpson stated that, "There is a desire for many young readers to read these classics, but their reanimation in the graphic novel brings these barriers down, especially for male readers."[19]

Simpson, too, cites nostalgia as a reason for his life-long interest in comic books and in *Paradise Comics'* accomplishments. Their understanding of nostalgia is translated into a measure of the sustainment of literacy and community surrounding *Paradise Comics*. Simpson adds, "Parents identify with a book or character they may have read as children. We can point them in the way of that same character or suggest titles with a similar take."[20] He recommended that, "Perhaps at one time the gender breakdown of customers was 90% male and 10% female, but this has shifted to 65% male and 35% female."[21] A statistic he attributes to the wider nature of appeal from some peripherals as video games and other media. The male reader is still in the majority, as he enjoys stories of contextual language, word and image synthesis, street jargon intertwined with proper English, and questions which his own persona might venture to ask, that begin with "What if?" and "What would it be like if I . . . . ?" Simpson believes that even as we traverse our future, the graphic novel, using its arch-story-telling structure, taps back into history and society, allowing the reader to remember where he came from.[22] At *Paradise Comics*, the knowledge of the pantheon of titles and stories offers an atmosphere the collector can savour, and the parent can trust. This store, too, has signings, and that is very attractive for all interested parties in the genre, as it opens the world behind the book, where the creator can shake hands with the reader!

There is an appreciable intangible to the atmosphere of the comic book store: that is the sense of community and belonging. This social mechanism at the micro level is connecting with one's fellow enthusiasts or the professional who knows all about the genre or at the macro level a connection to society in general and a sense that the individual, no matter who they are, become a relevant piece of the equation. Sean Clement, the weekend manager of my community comic book store, *The Comic Room*, suggested that, "There has been an evolution in the development of the audience of these books that, while at the elementary level, the superheroes, and titles like *Ink Heart* and *Bone* remain supreme, but then an adolescent hiatus takes place, with the return of the male reader in his twenties perhaps led by nostalgia and a sense that comic books can be cool again."[23] Mr. Clement who, like myself, is also a teacher, noted that, "At his Board (T.D.S.B.) many librarians are becoming in tune with the reading styles of boys and ESL/ELL students, lauding such titles as the aforementioned Bone, plus books like *Scott Pilgrim, The Wizard of Oz*, and Amulet."[24] Stores like the *Comic Room* bridge that gap between home and school. The voice of the creators also lends itself to an understanding of the significance of community in this form of literacy.

The weavers of image and prose, the comic book artists, also concur with the notion that it is as much as the genre itself, that the context of their purchase delivers that fourth dimension of meaning to the literacy experience. Artist Marvin Law stated that, "The modern draw for children to comic books is their link to the peripheral media and communities in which they reside."[25] He continued, "Reading comic books is as much a physical as a behavioural one, where a less imposing, heavy text treatment is supplanted by a captions-based approach which ultimately leads to a love of writing, and therein, a method and means which establishes a mindset that desires to make external connections with more of an accelerated pace than traditional text-based novella."[26] These very connections to external media, text, and experience represent a critical paradigm, which feeds the continued operation of the comic book store. It is entirely possible that one location ensures that these connections continue to accelerate the connectedness of this genre and its inextricable purveyance into all facets of memory and experience. Artist Kurt Lehner (Disney, Dream Works, Warner Brothers, and Marvel Comics) commented that, "The cool factor goes far beyond that of an appreciation of the images of the comic book, but evolves with a sense of self-identification or deep personification of the narrative and how the characters are in many respects extensions of children's imaginations and even laudable moral goals."[27] While the publishing and media houses may weave the dream, the comic book store casts the spell, taking the dream and transforming it into the fabric which the written word is vaulted into the mind and experience of the reader. Shane Kirschenblatt (*Dorothy Gale Journey to Oz, Star Wars* art) remarked that, "The appreciation and power of pure fantasy cannot be denied when such works are the literary sparks of the imagination and the passions, as aggressive heroism coins an age where text and media are fairly free flowing, the aspirations of youth find much in the confidence and possibilities of the heroic triumph in their own lives."[28] Thus, the literary atmosphere stokes that hopeful and youthful sense of possibilities and newness to the universe that certainly draws out the enthusiasm of the would-be reader. What is ultimately powerful is that some of those aspirations and realities have come off the written page into the real physical plane of existence.

The fascinating relationship between the promotion of literacy, media content, virtual community space, and physical geographic social space continues to shape the multi-paradigm-driven world of the comic book store. Given the dynamic of the virtual-spatial-temporal community, have comic book stores become the fulcrum driving the new media literacy mind and community space of the 21st Century? Arguably, yes, if the premise resides with the notion that one's sense of community and connectedness can reside in virtual, physical, and self-defined temporal time and space. These evolving building blocks of the new literacy everything from the printed word to the interpretive image, to the Hollywood film are drawn to the nexus of the comic book store, rife for plucking by the discerning reader to take and frame their own meanings and sense of community around them. These stores weave their magic and continue to prosper from an inherent and explicit knowledge of the virtual-spatial-temporal community of media and modern literacy. The new literary turn has indeed occurred, beguilingly as it might be, it began some eighty years ago, but through innovation, reinvention, and alternate framing by successive generations and media, it has evolved from a text-to-human perspective (planet to moon) to one which is more akin to a galaxy and all of its stars. No longer is the connectedness merely between the text and reader, but between the reader and inputs that exist in the realm of time, space, virtual space, and in their defined sense of community and modern media literacy. Were we to find a bright spot at the center of this new literary universe, it would be with the fantastic world of the comic book store and its respective owners, who hold the keys to their literacy realms in hand.

1 Manning, Matthew K.; Dolan, Hannah, ed. (2010). "1980s". DC Comics Year By Year A Visual Chronicle. <u>Dorling Kindersley</u>. p. 218. <u>ISBN</u> <u>978-0-7566-6742-9</u>. "The heroes of the DC Universe got a little more exposed thanks to the new ongoing effort Secret Origins, a title offering new interpretations to the backgrounds of some of comics' biggest icons."

2 <u>http://www.newkadia.com/?Official Handbook of the Marvel Universe Comic-Books=1111122326</u>, accessed on February 15, 2013, published 2000-13.

3 <u>http://www.paradisecomics.com</u>, published by Paradise Comics, 2010, accessed on January 12, 2013.

4 Joe Kilmartin (manager of The Comic Book Lounge and Gallery, Toronto), interview by Manfred von Vulte, December 8, 2012.

5 Joe Kilmartin (manager of The Comic Book Lounge and Gallery, Toronto), interview by Manfred von Vulte, December 8, 2012.

6 Joe Kilmartin (manager of The Comic Book Lounge and Gallery, Toronto), interview by Manfred von Vulte, December 8, 2012.

7 Joe Kilmartin (manager of The Comic Book Lounge and Gallery, Toronto), interview by Manfred von Vulte, December 8, 2012.

8 George Zotti (an owner of The Silver Snail, Toronto), interview by Manfred von Vulte, January 22, 2013.

9 George Zotti (an owner of The Silver Snail, Toronto), interview by Manfred von Vulte, January 22, 2013.

10 George Zotti (an owner of The Silver Snail, Toronto), interview by Manfred von Vulte, January 22, 2013.

11 George Zotti (an owner of The Silver Snail, Toronto), interview by Manfred von Vulte, January 22, 2013.

12 George Zotti (an owner of The Silver Snail, Toronto), interview by Manfred von Vulte, January 22, 2013.

13 George Zotti (an owner of The Silver Snail, Toronto), interview by Manfred von Vulte, January 22, 2013.

14 George Zotti (an owner of The Silver Snail, Toronto), interview by Manfred von Vulte, January 22, 2013.

15 George Zotti (an owner of The Silver Snail, Toronto), interview by Manfred von Vulte, January 22, 2013.

16 George Zotti (an owner of The Silver Snail, Toronto), interview by Manfred von Vulte, January 22, 2013.

17 Doug Simpson (manager of Paradise Comics, Toronto), interviewed by Manfred von Vulte, January 11, 2013.

18 Doug Simpson (manager of Paradise Comics, Toronto), interviewed by Manfred von Vulte, January 11, 2013.

19 Doug Simpson (manager of Paradise Comics, Toronto), interviewed by Manfred von Vulte, January 11, 2013.

20 Doug Simpson (manager of Paradise Comics, Toronto), interviewed by Manfred von Vulte, January 11, 2013.

21 Doug Simpson (manager of Paradise Comics, Toronto), interviewed by Manfred von Vulte, January 11, 2013.

22 Doug Simpson (manager of Paradise Comics, Toronto), interviewed by Manfred von Vulte, January 11, 2013.

23 Sean Clement (weekend manager of The Comic Room, Scarborough), interviewed by Manfred von Vulte, December 2, 2012.

24 Sean Clement (weekend manager of The Comic Room, Scarborough), interviewed by Manfred von Vulte, December 2, 2012.

25 Marvin Law (comic book artist, North York), interviewed by Manfred von Vulte, January 15, 2013.

26 Marvin Law (comic book artist, North York), interviewed by Manfred von Vulte, January 15, 2013.

27 Kurt Lehner (comic book artist, Disney, Dream Works, Warner Brothers, and Marvel Comics, North York), interviewed by Manfred von Vulte, February 13, 2013.

28 Shane Kirschenblatt (comic book artist Dorothy Gale Journey to Oz, North York), interviewed by Manfred von Vulte, February 13, 2013.

Literacy Dons a Cape and Comes to Canada

Teachers are always looking for innovative programs that address the multiple levels of ability and differentiation found in every classroom. Language Arts is a discipline where the range of student abilities has a tremendous scope, and often some intricate variables. The engaging nature of the Comic Book Project and Comics Go Global offers a new avenue into the development and progression of reluctant readers and writers, as well as enhancing the classroom experience for voracious readers and prolific writers. Enveloped in the power of the imagination and the crucible of media literacy, this initiative taps into the artist in all of us and will work wonders in the classroom, for all students.

When you have a student body that is high energy, very tactile and physical, with equally vigorous and energetic personalities, you'd better be prepared to keep up! As a Language Arts teacher at Northmount School, an independent, all-boys elementary school in North York, Ontario, I set my sites in early 2012 on enhancing the Language Arts program with something that would capture my students' imaginations—something with an inventive element.

Some of our boys are voracious readers, taking up to seven library books out at a time—but there are others who would not be reading independently were it not mandated by the Language Arts curriculum. My students are typically not interested in the nuances of relationships or ad nauseam descriptions as found in many of the novels touted to be excellent for junior and middle school readers (*Tuck Everlasting, Little Women*); instead they revel in stories about action. Role-playing games, *Choose Your Own Adventure* books, *Warhammer*, and other stylized activities and books reign supreme.

Into this amalgam came the idea of a comic book club. Having been a collector since I was nine years old, I wondered if the same zeal and enjoyment for these books might still exist with today's children. Out of a population of 93 Grade 3 to Grade 8 students, a third joined the Comic Book Club. Clearly, I had struck a vein of potential gold!

In our Language Arts program, students learn the skills of inference, prediction, summarization, making connections, and character construction and motivation, which allow them to discover the world behind the book. Fascinatingly, I discovered that many of our comic book readers were already using this skill set.

As we, in the Comic Book Club, exchanged our various *Spiderman, X-Men, Superman*, and *Avengers* books, I observed that even some very reluctant readers remained absolutely silent and thoroughly focused. I asked a number of these students questions regarding plot, character, mood, theme, and complex vocabulary, while also employing terms like antagonist and protagonist. The responses exceeded my expectations. Recently, I interviewed Joe Kilmartin of the *Comic Book Lounge and Gallery*. When I shared my observations of my students, he commented: "With the world becoming very media/visually literate, someone who is learning English could use the comic book, engaging a sense of prediction and revision at the same time, by following sequential design, yet being able to flip back and restore the immediate visual hit again and again."

The students played out scenarios in their minds and with their peers, engaging the higher-capacity thinking skills of analysis, synthesis, prediction and evaluation. But there was still a missing piece in this tremendous literacy experience.

The design of a comic book was the natural end goal of this literacy initiative. Students had only been expanding on the written word and the worlds fashioned by other authors; it was time they struck out and constructed their own fantastic realms.

Comic books had fueled their imaginations and provided a basis for writing to commence. Now I needed a program that would suit both reluctant and prolific writers. The popular Internet-based programs *Bit Strips* and *Go Animate* were good starting points. They structured the students' mindset in regards to how sequential thinking and writing looked in a more dynamic form than their comic books, but they lacked the much-needed organizational infrastructure that powers graphic novels and comics. I searched the Internet for a program that would fill this missing gap, and I found it in Dr. Michael Bitz's Comic Book Project/Comics Go Global initiative. Created in 2001 in partnership with Columbia University and Dark Horse Comics, the program, designed as a means to bring creativity back into children's lives, recently became its own entity within the Centre for Educational Pathways in New York City. It can be found all through the U.S., in the United Kingdom, New Zealand, Australia, and now at Northmount School, its first school in Canada!

The Comic Book Project/Comics Go Global was truly that missing piece of best practice. Each student is given a character guide that narrows the creation process, and character creation is accomplished by the use of t-charts and other diagrams. Elements of graphic organizers are used to structure and storyboard the narrative, while blocking out each of the scenes. Participants are guided by the efforts of the organizing teacher and through satellite conferences with Dr. Bitz and other global participants who edit, guide, and share their work. Students then receive a 12-page booklet, closely resembling a comic book but with a blank cover and rectangles of varying sizes on the inside pages. The students' stories unfold through these pages. The final edit of each student's creation will be published on the Comic Book Project's website. This publishing component, along with the global conferencing with other students, comprises the "Comics Go Global" side of the program.

This program was a masterful addition to the series we were already using, *Six plus One Writing Traits and Spectrum Writing*. Essentially, participants learn sequential planning, thinking, and writing in a cloak of imagination and inspiration. The process of scaffolding writing ideas, using vocabulary lists (comic books have a high incidence of complex words), and graphic organizers found within the aforementioned programs and in Comics Go Global proved to be invaluable. While Internet-based programs perhaps provided a spark of novelty, this program tapped into the three pillars of boys' enthusiasm for writing and reading: relevancy, duration, and exposure. Weekly conferences via Skype to New York and with our partner class in Indiana created a constant resurgence in passion for the project. Whenever technology can be incorporated into the writing process, it accelerates the desire of students to participate. Excitement reached a fever pitch when both Global Television and the Space Channel came to cover the Comic Book Project and our Skype sessions, and broadcast our project across Canada! Ultimately, the students' comic books will be published online for the whole world to see. Truly the three pillars of boys' enthusiasm were satisfied, as were many curricular tenets of media literacy.

While the videoconferences were the crescendo of the week's work, the story talk and idea sharing amongst the participants were truly the idea factories in motion.

In many respects, the Comic Book Project is a summative of sorts. It combines all of the strands, proficiencies and competencies of our Language Arts program, in a format that allows students to be the architects of their own worlds. What makes it truly unique is the thought and scaffolding behind the narrative of the comic book. While the videoconferences were the crescendo of the week's work, the story talk and idea sharing amongst the participants were truly the idea factories in motion. I witnessed collaborative efforts, peer-to-peer critique without negative emotion or reaction, and the genuine application of higher-order thinking skills—not in some teacher-led discussion and response sequence, but rather occurring in independent and unsupported student application and learning. There was also a lot of fun taking place—the smiles and sound effects said it all. Our boys really got into their stories and began proposing the typical "what-if" scenarios and humorous accounts. They enjoyed designing their first comic book cover, using exemplars from the comic book club and their own collections to guide their way. A great deal of time was spent on the covers, as they also established their antagonists and protagonists there. Once through to the main body of the book, they stopped and worked on graphic organizers, so their stories would, as Mark D., in Grade 3, said, "Be really action packed and most of all, be understandable to the whole world!" After this, the panels, rich in text, imagery, and quality of vocabulary and story, began to be unveiled. It was an awesome sight when the prolific writer consulted with the reluctant reader on how to make his book shine, and truly spectacular when the voracious reader informed the reluctant writer that he had enjoyed his work. Yes, there is still very much a sense of wonder and magic in the pages of comic books—and now its readers have learned to cast their own spells.

Beyond the Comic Book and then Back: Taking Reluctant Readers through the Double Helix of Literacy

There is always a sense of satisfaction when we finally see our children reading, especially when they have been deemed reluctant readers. The phrase that is most often heard, "Well, at least they are reading!" Granted, a milestone has been reached. This cannot be underestimated or relegated to a natural stepping stone that would have ultimately occurred. The difficult truth remains that if a student is not encouraged or driven to read, the process can be markedly protracted with episodes of stagnation and loss of competency with the development of literacy and comprehension. Thus, while there is much to celebrate when a reluctant reader begins to find an interest in reading, which is akin to the germination of a seed. If one wishes a child to flourish that initial spark needs to be stoked, so that a competent student can be forged. The question remains, how then do we progress our children beyond that initial "Big Bang" effect? At the heart of the issue is a required acceptance that reading is a long-term temporal construct that requires all stakeholders to recognize that while short-term solutions may affect change (tutoring, differentiated instruction, moments of intervention, and academic accommodations) the genuine drive to move forward rests in the frequency and consistency of the aforementioned short-term solutions acting in concert with each other inside, and perhaps more importantly, outside of the course and classroom experience. Much like the broad consensus regarding student success: an interested and active parent in education equals high performance; so too, the same active and interventionist oversight is required.

Ultimately, our children should be able to gain the techniques required to see and interpret the world behind the book. To take hold of a text and deconstruct it based on a set of criteria inherent to their ability to read and evaluate/synthesise material. As a laudable goal, this is undoubtedly the end game. The items listed below are the bridges across that great gulf from first contact to mastery. Be warned, be cautious, and be patient, the transference of literacy to a level beyond cursory entertainment-based reading does work in tandem with the passing of time, the development of scholastic skills, and something that cannot be disregarded, the evolution of personality, maturity and life experience that ebbs and flows along an intersecting continuum, not a straight line. Perhaps the former is the factor which most acts as a governor switch on the development of literacy.

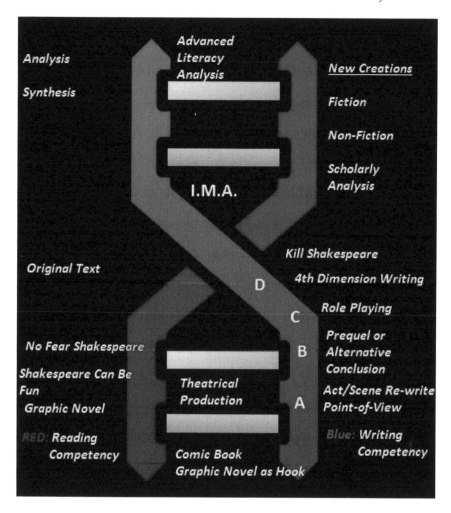

Changing Editions

Parents may wish to begin with a text that is highly illustrated, but short on words. This works extremely well with many of the classics. Take for instance Robert Louis Stevenson's *Treasure Island*. One can purchase the Dover Thrift Edition which is largely text-based and not a good transference point for the reluctant reader. However, with the Sterling Illustrated Classic's version, one reviewer was spot on in his assessment: "A *great book to introduce classics to young readers.*

Robert Ingpen's illustrations greatly assist young readers in understanding this classic of 19th century literature. There are 70 brilliant watercolor illustrations appropriately scattered throughout the book which greatly assist young readers in following the story line." Many male readers need a visualization of what is occurring in the text to make it "real" for themselves. These visual cues and chunked information make a difference in their approach to the text. Don't be afraid to begin with versions that are geared to a much younger reader and quickly progress up the line. Building the exoskeleton of meaning and then later giving meat to the bones is a valid and successful approach.

Selecting Books that Explain the Narrative: Shaking up Shakespeare

One of the most daunting texts a student will come across is any work by William Shakespeare. The reluctant reader will almost immediately throw up a road block to the Bard because the language of Elizabethan England proved to be too befuddling when it came to comprehending the story. If ever there was a tome of writing that required illustration it is certainly Shakespeare. The graphic novels are certainly available to guide one through these iconic tales. They are most certainly not the condensed, serialized format of the comic book, but rather longer and illustrated treatments. Where do we go after the graphic novel? Two of the best guides for Shakespeare are the Lois Burdett series *Shakespeare Can be Fun* and the Spark Notes series, *The No Fear Shakespeare.*

Burdett fashions such classics as *Hamlet* and *Macbeth* in modern English, but selects critical quotes from both works to guide the reader. Illustrations by the students who actually worked with Burdett are found throughout the books and make for both an entertaining read, but also help to refocus the reader. The drawings also convey the message, "If I can do it, so can you." Acting out scenes with my Grade 5 class came easy, because the text lends itself to doing that. I read Burdett's version of *Macbeth* with my Grade 8 class, before tackling a more comprehensive text.

The Spark Notes series, *The No Fear Shakespeare*, is not structured like the abridged "*Coles* or *Cliff Notes*" format, which may come to mind based on the name of the publisher. Nothing untoward against the C and C format, but that type of textual assistance should be a last resort, if not a finishing tool, after the proper avenues of learning have been utilized. However, they are brilliant at providing charts identifying the aliases which Shakespeare's characters have. It is still critical that the readers, even of daunting text, experience and frame the narrative for themselves. *The No Fear Shakespeare* has a simple, yet highly effective methodology: Elizabethan English on the left and modern English on the right, line-for-line. With plenty of discussion and role playing lessons, Shakespeare becomes quite enjoyable and a favourite amongst students.

Part of the transference from the comic book or graphic novel to alternative/mainstream textual treatment is how the teacher then takes the text and enacts innovative lessons and assignments with the material. A rather imaginative tactic has been to play around with the idea of Point-of-View (1.8 Language Arts Curriculum, Ontario) in written and oral presentations. Students might be asked to re-write an Act or Scene from another character's point-of-view. Imagine what Hamlet would read like if it were from his diabolical Uncle Claudius' view? Deeper levels of comprehension can now be charted:

Level A: A re-write of an Act or Scene, based on another character's point-of-view.

Level B: The writing of another act or alternate conclusion.

Level C: Playing the character from the scene with original dialogue.

Level D: Using the cannon of the story, then assuming a character's strengths and limitations to interact with other such characters in a world students create: ***Reading in the Fourth Dimension***.

There exists a marvelous adaptation of Level D in, what else, but a graphic novel! Enter *Kill Shakespeare*! Having met the creators/ writers of this body of work at the 2012 Toronto Comic Con, the wit and intelligence of Conor McCreery, Anthony Del Col and Andy Belanger certainly come through on the pages of their graphic novel series. However, it is not another treatment of Shakespeare via the aforementioned methods, but truly an example of high order comprehension and metacognition taken to its limits. For the uninitiated, the characters of many Shakespearean works now exist in one universe, acting together and forging new relationships and motivations from jumping off points of recognition with implicit and subtle references to the original text, but also exercising a sense of literal free will or desire for literal free will against their creator, Shakespeare himself. More I shall not say it is definitely worth the read. However, this graphic novel does not function like the typical comic book or graphic novel in the reluctant reader sequence of comprehension development, rather than complete a hermeneutic circle of meaning it creates, if you will, a double helix hermeneutic continuum, which vaults the reader into an even deeper level of metacognition, even more complex than ***Reading in the Fourth***

Dimension. It is perhaps the conduit required before reading non-fictional literary analysis of Shakespearean text.

Three Steps Forward, One Step back

Always encourage reading. Don't be mortified if your son is bringing home some of the "giants" of the elementary literacy world, like *Captain Underpants, Bone*, and *Diary of a Whimpy Kid;* these titles are just fine, but should not be the sole source of reading material. Think of reading like exercising at a fitness club. There are some people who just sign up for the gym and go all out: they lift a ton of weights, and are never seen again because of a massive muscle strain or lack of pacing. Literacy is just the same. What a child reads is often levelled. There will be books below, at, and above their capacity and skill sets. While they will breeze through some light titles, they will want to read books with more substance, as well. This is the mind in training. I will often see students walking out of our library with one of the *Lord of the Rings* trilogy with a most determined look on their face. The majority of these students will read through some of the chapters, and then put the book down for a long time. However, they will revisit it, perhaps not during the current academic year, but they will come back to it. This is the perfect time for a parent or teacher to intervene and suggest some shorter titles that are still within the ability of the reader.

Big Picture, Big Themes

Educators and parents often struggle with this very open-ended question, "What type of things do you like to read about?" Your typical male elementary school student will reply: "I don't know, aliens, action, cars, mystery, things like that." The spectre of frustration might begin to raise its head. However, try digging deeper. Ask what specific books your children liked that they have read. Then try to discern some overall theme that these books possess. Avoid specificity with that process. Look for themes such as the following: courage, teamwork, good vs. evil, struggle, mystery, survival, and discovery. It is guaranteed that at least one of these themes exists in your child's reading experience. Then begin to source some books with these themes. This process will also work if the child is interested in a particular subject, geographical location, point in history, technological item, or dynamic product. As an example, my Grade 3 class read a brilliant book called *Varjak Paw*. It is about a young cat that must go out into the dangerous underground world of cats in New York City in order to help his family that is being kept prisoner. The book is filled with the aforementioned themes, very light on illustration, heavier in text, but rich in thematic connections and points of interest for reluctant readers who seek action and a swift moving plot. Readers will want to act out parts of the book, develop posters, and perhaps even comic strips, based on a chapter or two. One of the keys to accelerated reading and writing prowess lies in these mid-range texts that engage the reader in fewer than 300 pages.

Memory as Muscle

There is something inherent in being able to hold a book and immediately go back to verify the information of text on previous pages. Whether this occurs with the traditional printed text or in digital format is currently under some debate. However, the fact remains that memory and connection play a key role in developing one's ability to read, connect, analyze, and synthesize. The comic book and graphic novel have a splendid manner in introducing such a skill set in a rather implicit in innocuous way. The readers can go back to any plot point and instantly refresh their short-term memory with a vivid image married to text. ***With the world becoming very media/***

visually literate, someone who is learning English or a reluctant reader/writer could use the comic book as a means of engaging a sense of prediction and revision at the same time, by following sequential design, yet being able to visually flip back and restore the immediate visual hit again and again. This **informed memory access** (I.M.A.) and renewal is at the heart of the means to learn English in its colloquial and contextual element, while discerning the culture from which it had been derived in a parallel process to the native English speaker, defining the world of the comic book, which for the ESL/ELL learner includes the new world of his country. Once the reluctant readers have strengthened their I.M.A. they can proceed to heavier text-driven narratives and use this competency bequeathed to them by comic books to become a stronger reader.

To think of learning to read as linear progression of ability would not be entirely correct. On the surface, reading appears as a maturation process. While persons might begin with simple picture books with no text, and progress to novella, and further to what is deemed higher order literacy, that progression, while appearing linear, should not be assessed as being such a "given" in human development. Reading does evolve through time, yet the faculty for reading above a rudimentary and cursory level is dependent upon the quality of the intervention and management of texts and their deconstruction occurs from outside influences. Thus, if a student was left to their own devices and continuously handed texts, their development and skill sets regarding literacy may not develop on a linear scale of positive progression. In short, they might stall, stop and, worst of all, cease reading as it has become too cumbersome and difficult to progress to weightier texts. Proficiency and enthusiasm can be revived through the techniques and strategies posited in this article. Never let it be said that this revival can engage a variety of texts and go below and beyond a reader's current ability. While we all want our children to read beyond the comic book and graphic level, we cannot sweep these texts aside while we pursue what we feel are higher classics and literary treatments. Literacy is not a continuum existing on a straight line, but rather a double helix, twisting and turning through time, revisiting and renewing old competencies while striving to enter new gateways to the future. Fascinatingly, the framing of comic books and graphic novels as a jumping-off point to literacy is a correct assumption; however, the genre seems to reinvent itself and reoccur offering new aptitudes and proficiencies at gateways of development along the double helix continuum of literacy.

Part Two

—The Innovative Classroom—

Inside the Successful Classroom:
My World at School

The classroom is a fish bowl. Parents and students can peer in at any time and discover a unique world. As students will spend more waking hours at school, then their residence; the class should parallel the values of the home and engage the student in responsible, critical, and imaginative thought. We often fail to see the school and its rooms as a living space, but given the time and interaction within these places, they certainly are. The worlds of school and home tend to be regarded as two solitudes in the mind of the student and being so, never the two shall meet. It has been my experience that: if what is generally mirrored in the home is expected in the school, then student achievement will certainly increase. My grandmother had a relevant saying in regards to this, "Show me an orderly room, and I will show you an orderly person with an equally orderly mind." The classroom sets up this significant virtue.

Have you ever seen a school with graffiti on its outside walls or perhaps one whose classrooms are messy and in a state of disrepair? Fascinatingly, some of the children that belong to those schools are in similar physical and mental states. The schools, which are successful, instil their students a sense of pride in the institution. However, school spirit can only go so far. Witness any school during the last decade whose custodial staff went on strike. The crucial step forward from pride and spirit is the sense of responsibility and ownership. Children need to know that with responsibility comes freedom. The creation of classroom jobs and student councils motivates students to have a higher regard for their environment. If everyone is given a small measure of responsibility their daily environment can improve. This can be equally applied in the home. If clothes or wrappers are found around the house, an appropriate saying would be, "While it may not be your garbage, it is your house."

The classroom should engage and inspire the student. There is a fine line however, between this and amusement. Your children are not going to school to be entertained. Students should have a classroom that showcases excellence in work, has a representative space for every child to demonstrate the "gifts" they offer, and utilize the entire spatial area with captivating images and charts that "scaffold learning" so youth can reach even higher levels of achievement and personal growth. There is always the chance that a room can appear like a garage sale gone wrong, but the conscientious teacher keeps the look fresh and non-static. Color also plays a critical role. Plain white walls communicate a sense of boredom and a lack of effort by all parties.

Green and blue are arguably the best colours to use because they convey concentration and a calm mood. Slight accents of red highlight critical information. Many parents will see dynamic teachers using "behaviour charts" on everything from daily manners to modelling proper listening and speaking. I often wonder if these charts shouldn't be in some homes.

Certainly the diversity of resources in a student's room can influence critical thinking and the ability to inference information. The Language Arts portion of the class should offer a wide diversity of texts from fiction to non-fiction. A student must be able to participate in read aloud sessions with his or her peers and also frequently present writing in an oral fashion while afterwards, placing the composition in a designated public space. Science and Social Studies would benefit greatly from the myriad of striking posters available. Experiments, samples, and replicas on display and in reach of curious hands bring about a whole new level of discovery through the senses and address the various learning styles of pupils including auditory, visual-spatial, and kinesthetic. The calming capacity of an aquarium and lush plant life affect both mood and experiential learning. This holds true for all subjects. The classroom is also about human life! Certainly a segment of the wall space should celebrate achievement, holidays, birthdays, and other special events. The joy of this world should not be left out in the hallway. If students and teachers can celebrate their best moments together surely empathy and love of learning will have fertile ground and its observation from inside and out will be well worth it.

The February Report Card
Might This Be the winter
of our Discontent?

The Government of Ontario will place public and separate elementary school teachers in a precarious position in February 2011. The old adage, "the road to ruin is paved with good intentions" might ring true in the ears of education administrators and teachers and only be drowned out by the actual phone calls they will receive when the first letter/numerical report cards of the year will arrive in the homes of students. The first report card of the year was comment based and designed to inform parents of progress, while not defining that progress on an empirical level, unless parents individually asked for a mark set or the individual school requested that teachers post numerical results in some fashion. Most did not. Why have we come to this position? Why might it be problematic?

The assessment piece in education is one of those factors that most teachers would not rank as one of the top five joys of their profession. It is fraught with difficulty and is one of the most political aspects of teaching. At its centre is the means by which progress can be measured over time. It answers the question, how is my child doing? It really conveys, how the child is dealing with the curriculum and if they are learning. The great paradox is whether to assess for learning, or conduct assessment of learning. The first method is the use of summative vehicles (tests, quizzes, assignments, projects) to teach students the curriculum. It is an outdated and inferior practice that creates 'trial by fire' scenarios where students either know the material or they discover their gaps too late in the reporting process. The latter, is the use of the same instruments to discover what students have learned at the end of a unit or at the culmination of a series of concepts. The student has many opportunities to gain mastery of a competency. To borrow an analogy from the sporting world; 'no harm, no foul' assignments are returned to the students with guiding comments that offer both suggestions and corrections with a dash of praise. The whole idea of formative assessment is so that a high level of competence can be achieved when the "real assessment (summative)" is given. If students receive only summative letter/numerical marks on each and every submission, they will become perpetually affixed to numbers and loose site over the value of the process (thinking and learning), while over-emphasizing the final result. A summative teaching philosophy also leads to a decline for a love of learning and discourages children who need time to master a concept. The great victory for the formative/summative process is that children are ultimately rewarded with a fine result after they have been encouraged by numerous attempts at proficiency. Should this hybrid then have been applied to report cards?

The report card is the ultimate summative piece. The revamped model is essentially taking the formative model of assessment and applying it to a higher level then perhaps necessary. Formative assessment should not be co-opted into appearing as a summative model. Problematic to this position is that there exists a multi-generational dynamic that has become part of the social fabric of emotion and understanding in regards to education. Parents want to see specific results. While they understand the role of formative practices within the term, they want to see exactly how their children are faring. This is because generations of Canadians, including the current one that is in elementary school, have been assessed on report cards with letter or numerical grades. There is an understanding in the community of memory of society what these results mean. The whole system will collapse in semantics and the application.

If a child receives the comment 'progressing well' then what is the interpretation of that mark for the student and their parent(s), this is incredibly subjective. If the comment was the highest one available, then what is the true mark? A defined result will exist within the mind of the assessed. The crisis for teachers will occur when the system reverts back to the classic summative model and a numerical or letter grade will now appear. Grades will be challenged and there will be a new accountability of numerical results required to justify the grade on the February report. The other issue is that the application of formative comments will appear vague to many families who do not understand the nuances of the English language or those of the noble efforts of educators to be inclusive of the formative process on report cards. Ideally, if there would exist universality to replacing all alphanumerical summative report cards with the process orientated commentary of the formative model; this would improve the quality of elementary school reporting. This paradigm shift will not ever occur because secondary and post-secondary institutions hold letter/numerical grading sacrosanct to their operation and legal feedback to their students. If the whole education system does not change, change will not come and friction will result.

Assessment of learning through comment heavy formative practices with opportunities for success for all different types of learners is without question presently defined as 'best practice' within the profession. If the government is going to create an initial report card that is a hybrid of the formative and summative process, they must be aware that the stakeholders in this assessment process, namely the parents, are viewing this through their own paradigm of assessment history, which has for them explicit and implicit interpretations of achievement and failure. Some education specialists would suggest that for every numerical grade there must exist a specific set of rubric standards, meaning that 69 have slightly different points of achievement than 70. Parents do not make this distinction. They do, however, have a clearer picture if the summative mark is a specific number or even a letter represented by a numerical range instead of a comment such as 'progressing with some difficulty.'

Fall report cards; even though they might be based on a smaller sample of summative assessments give parents a warning and a sense of how their child is doing early in the school year. A lack of specificity until February is going to cause all parties a great deal of consternation. While the universality of reporting would be perfect, it cannot be achieved. A return to three summative reports, with the addition of clear formative 'best practice' influence, might be the answer. Summative report cards that grow in value from 20% to 30% to 50% successively through each term are a practical solution. The final report card would publish a third term mark and a final mark, which would be determined by the aforementioned percent breakdown. Parents would accept a report card that has many formative suggestions, but would give them the specificity they understand and can work with. This would ring true for everyone.

Decoding Male Communication: Understanding what a boy is saying— even when he isn't talking

During the past ten years, much has been written regarding the education of boys and how they act. "Girl behaviour became the gold standard," according to *Raising Cain* coauthor Michael Thompson. "Boys are treated like defective girls."

However, the language and emotional attachment boys utilize in different social situations is well worth taking a look at. Research psychologist Leonard Sax argued that schools needed to address the social behaviours of boys and adapt learning environments and teaching practices to their gender specific actions. Boys have a unique language of their own and it will often be misunderstood as malicious, careless, non-serious or at best foolish and indifferent.

RAISING BOYS OF HONOUR
A COLUMN BY MANFRED VON VULTE

Author Jim Stenson put it this way, "Getting to know a boy is like looking at a roughly kept home with an untended garden and a make-shift fence; however, once the door to the home is opened, a beautiful interior can be found." Having taught at Northmount School, an all-boys elementary school in North York for ten years (and as Vice Principal for two), I can set forth some tangible examples of the gender specific language and reactions of male students, to help further understanding.

Here are some specific situations that arise with boys only:

It seemed like a good idea at the time.

This comment usually occurs once personal or property damage has taken place. The best of intentions has them to disaster. Boys tend to be impulsive and often lack the thought patterns to determine short and long-term effects and consequences. While boosting their friend to retrieve a stuck basketball was a good idea, the unintended result of a bent pole or ill-conceived safety net has delivered a less than satisfactory ending.

Sir! Johnny is paralysed from the neck down out on the field!

Boys have a tremendous tendency toward injury; some stress avoidance at any cost, others revel in risk, while the majority tend to wear injuries as a badge of courage. Prior to their social parade as heroic pariah, each and every injury is often portrayed by them and their peers as a major code blue trauma. It's really part of the male mystique and also how much they can shock a supervisory teacher. Every exaggerated comment results in a miraculous recovery. Johnny was up and running is less than two minutes, but he and his peers have had their moment in the sun.

Come quick, Johnny is choking for no reason at all!

Can you spot the exaggeration and the element of truth? Johnny is indeed choking and this must be dealt with first; however, the messenger is covering up something. Boys will be quick to point out an emergency. They will also try to cover any prohibitive behaviour in their initial call for help hoping you might forget the quick admission of guilt. Ninety per cent of the time, Johnny has recovered on his own and all that is left to be determined was the reason. In this case spit balls through a pen went in reverse.

Somebody stole my pencil and hid my binder!

There is in every school in our nation a terrible thief, vandal, and bully; his name is ``somebody. `` They may even be in your home or office. In actual fact their real name is Order, first name Lack Of. Male students are very possessive and proud of the space given to them. However, these parameters, when not enforced lead to a type of Manifest Destiny. The thinking goes like this, ``My desk is in my classroom, I can put my books near my desk, the books near my desk are close to the shelf, I can place my material there too.`` Before long, something has gone missing and the culprit is SOMEBODY!

There not laughing at me, their laughing near me.

No one enjoys being the butt of a joke, but with young men the nuances of this are fascinating. They do not mind being the class clown, and having their peers laugh at them. They also do not mind laughing with the class at themselves. However, boys do not like to be laughed at. Any point of pride or weakness, prelude to a consequence, or result of a (physical or mental) fall will result in upset feelings.

Is everything okay? How about now? Okay how about now?

If you simply stop at the first question nothing will be revealed. After some time passes and the tell-tale quivering upper lip and slightly vibrating chin, the doors of upset will open. Boys will take a much longer time to communicate their emotional pain. This is totally different than with their physical wounds. However, once those doors are open and the waterworks have begun, listen with great empathy and wait until the young man has come up with some of his own solutions. Your contributions will then be receptive, innovative and wise. Boys need trust and time to reveal their emotional pain and DO seek solutions.

Sir, I didn't do the homework because I didn't get it.

A good teacher will set their homework policy from day one for male students. I usually say that if an incompletion occurs, come with a note or see me before the homework check takes place, not during. This creates a fine dynamic of honesty and allows for a generally punitive free class, but with all of the responsibility and sound learning intact. The work must still get done. I have a theory that not understanding homework and admitting to it is directly linked to the male adult behaviour of not seeking medical attention until its often too late. Bottom line parents, saying, "I don't know is the first step to knowledge."

Associative Thinking

When asked what a leper was by the Priest, (a proud hand was raised) "A leper is a large black cat similar to a puma."

"Sir, when I die will I really see Satan?"

(Response-Teacher) *"Of course you will see all of the saints, even Saint Ann."*

(Pause with trepidation), *"Sir Will I really see Satan?"*

Boys will often use this type of reasoning with oral and written communication as they are goal oriented for a response. They will associate their own knowledge rapidly with what you expect of them. Have them slow down, consider what they are saying, and rather than skim their text or thoughts teach them to devote time to them.

Certainly more examples exist to illustrate male communication patterns and how to understand and modify teaching and parenting practices to them. However raising a young man requires four critical tenants: understanding, patience, parameters and a flexible sense of humour.

As much as education has modified itself for female success over the past twenty years, so too, must the pendulum swing back to do justice to male students. Boys communicate for effect, the rapid transfer of ``unedited`` information and to convey emotion through coded speech. Like their female counterparts, they want your attention and your time—two gifts any parent of any means can provide their child. If the opportunity arises again and a young man relays his story to you listen intently then look for the code behind boys' communication. Then a door to a beautiful interior will surely open.

Fish Tales:
A Boy Encounters Responsibility

As I was walking through the halls of Northmount, I had noticed that Mr. Ruch (Grade 4) had purchased an aquarium for his classroom. I stopped in to see what kind of gravel and filter he had acquired. An aquarium guy is always curious about such details. As I passed by, each successive hour revealed his science students dutifully cleaning the gravel, filling the tank with water, and ultimately putting in an underwater plant. On one of his prep periods, I again dropped by and offered more advice about letting the water stand for at least forty-eight hours. When one is an aquarium hobbyist it tends to stay with you for life. I am sure Mr. Ruch knew all about the water, but I felt compelled to tell him anyway. To quote Shakespeare, many aquarium hobbyists have felt the bitter sting of the "slings and arrows of outrageous fortune" and lived the phrase "to be or not to be."

The year was 1982 and my mother offered my sister and me a very unique proposition. She wanted to buy us something educational in the form of lessons or some type of an experience. Immediately, my sister wanted piano lessons; as I can recall, some of her friends were already enrolled. I paused at the thought, not because I didn't like music, after all, I played the clarinet, but in typical male fashion, I wanted something cool that some of my friends were really into doing. For a number of years before the great proposition, I had become enamoured with all things aquatic. Our local lake in Winnipeg was inhabited with Crayfish, and I recollect taking a number of them for pets, much to my mother's disgust or fear. On another occasion, a frog had *somehow* gotten onto a Winnipeg city bus and was wildly jumping around. I had chased it, even fishing it out of the purse of a rather surprised and unsuspecting senior citizen. Once we had moved to Toronto, several of my friends lived near a local creek, which was at the time, not yet ruined by the cement restructuring that would take place years later, destroying all of the wildlife. I know this comes as surprising by today's standards of safety, but my friends and I would often be down by the creek catching tadpoles destined for some pickle or jam jar at home. I do remember many of my friends' parents (mine included) ordering us to put the tadpoles back. I think they objected more to the smelly creek water that came with them and the elimination of any future use of the jars we kept them in. So my mother's offer in 1982 of course led to the purchase of my first aquarium. The amateur was now going pro!

I had marvelled at many of the fish tanks which some of my friends in the neighbourhood had. What was of particular interest to me, were the number of men (fathers of my friends) who encouraged the hobby with their sons and worked with them on it. Grand aquariums of tropical fish and other sea creatures abounded in their homes, but in retrospect, something else was happening. These friends of mine were learning responsibility and the transfer of knowledge from other males. Dr. Leonard Sax (*Boys Adrift*, 2007) laments the disappearance of this process as the "revenge of the forsaken gods." In my case, I had struck up a friendship with a neighbour who had asked me (through my mother) to take care of his place when he and his wife were in Quebec. Through my early teens, my neighbour and I shared this hobby together and lived through many die offs, population explosions, algae infestations, fish swaps, and constant upgrades of the world's we were building together. All the while, I was learning the tenets of responsibility required of every aquarium hobbyist. The short-term and long-term duty of this endeavour does educate its followers in efficient cleaning and caring for other living things. It also gave me the sense that life is not without complication, loss, and effort. Sadly, my "big brother" Mike died of Leukemia when I was fourteen and his wife and daughter moved back to Montreal. The adventures of childhood with the life aquatic and the knowledge bequeathed to me from my neighbour have lasted a lifetime. So upon viewing the grand old hobby being resurrected for another generation, I couldn't help but chime in. Perhaps the forsaken gods are not gone after all, as old Neptune casts a spell on another eager and inspired generation.

The Virtues and Social Graces of the Culinary Arts:
Discovering Passion, Patience, and Time

My grandmother was the world's greatest baker and cook. Even though she did not let me into the kitchen, I was able to glean enough technique from her to begin my own journey into the world of cuisine. I often wondered if she was laughing from above when she saw me in the kitchen at home, or at school working with the boys on preparing the latest baked goods. Born in 1908, Granny came from a part of Europe, that she used to say, was the same village, but belonged to at least four different countries/empires, before 1950. Her repertoire was grounded on the time-in-memorial traditions of the "Volks Deutsche" or ethnic Germans, which in her case, existed in an enclave south of what is now Bratislava, called Deutsche Proben. She was what later became known as a Carpathian German; few, if any, still exist in that part of Europe. When she arrived in Canada, in the early 1950's, the influences of all of the other great cultures of this land crept into her bailiwick of culinary art. As a child, I can recall her attentively sitting by the television set eagerly taking down the details of the recipes presented on numerous morning cooking programs, then later, serving them at our dinner table. We told her that she could write away for those details, but she preferred to get the information as it was presented. I would later marvel at this knowing that she came to Canada speaking no English, yet after less than two decades, could speak the language with little effort and even transfer audio to text from television. While I never became involved with her baking, she would hover around me with great concern and probably some amazement, that I was able to make some rudimentary meals of my own. She would teach my mother and when possible, my sister, some of the ins and outs of meal preparation. We were all educated in the fact that fine gastronomy required three key ingredients: passion, patience, and time. These tenets appear to be waning in our fast-paced, immediate gratification centered modern world, where perhaps, the book of recipes has been replaced by the telephone book.

In the film *Kate and Leopold*, the Duke of Albany (Leopold) commented that, "Without the culinary arts, the crudeness of life would be unbearable." I often wondered if this was some allusion lamenting the contraction of family meal time and the meaningful discussions therein, or perhaps even the end result of the current obesity crisis in children and adults. One of the finer gifts of our immigrant heritage as it may exist in our families as a living example, or even as a distant echo is the need to have some meals prepared in the household and eaten together. Being blessed with a grandmother who was at home and cooked is not the lot for every family in today's world, and the realities of life often circumvent the desires for one to eat healthy, or even together. However, the loss of these traditions need not be total. There are in our secondary and some middle schools, Home Economics classes that teach cooking and baking. Perhaps the knowledge of specific recipes may not remain with the student, but the desire and the confidence to prepare meals might just remain. Regrettably, these programs have been severely diminished at the elementary and secondary levels. Just as with Industrial Arts, Home Economics has suffered the limiting gaze of the academic stream, and been wrongly labelled as competencies that are regarded as menial, peripheral, and relegated to vocational.

The present generation of children may however turn the tide. The emerging knowledge base regarding food, from its growth to its preparation is with the consciousness of our youth. Many are unfortunately saddled with severe food allergies. Afflictions such as peanut (nut) and shellfish anaphylactic reactions, glutton and lactose intolerance, and allergies to eggs, fish, and chocolate have brought many parents back to the recipe books in an effort to control and dare I say, save the lives of their children. The marketplace cannot address a multitude of allergy restrictions in the food that is mass produced. Adolescents too, are realizing that healthy food choices and preparation are the keys to looking and feeling well. Ask any child to read the ingredients of their favourite chocolate bar or bag of chips, and there you have before you a home chemistry lesson. Learning to cook, places young people on the correct path. It is the way and means to learn patience, and for many, removes them from the despicable and dangerous path of body image and beauty that is sold to them by the fashion industry. I am hoping it will also change courtship amongst younger generations.

I have heard many good fathers give their daughters the following advice, "It's not what he says, but what he does." The majority of dating advice seems to be largely geared to women. What is often missing in this education of the novice male dater is how to be a gentleman. Young men should know their way around the kitchen. If meal preparation is truly passion, patience, and time, what better a metaphor than meal preparation from one's suitor or later, husband? The other similarities are quite evident. There will also come a time in a young man's life where his parents will not be around. My aunt in Calgary had a memorable expression in regards to this dilemma, "If you like to eat, just work backwards!" While rather humorous, this was quite true. The novelty of instant macaroni and cheese, hot dogs, and pizza wears off quickly in university. Given the litany of complaints from women in post-secondary schools about their male cohorts (he plays too many video games, there aren't enough quality men around, and he is a slob), these can be dispelled by a young man who can conjure up some things around the kitchen. A well-prepared meal, says a great deal without much being said. The lessons of the recipe should begin early in the life of a male child. Questions like, "How may I help?", become the hallmark of a young man who is beginning to familiarize himself with food preparation. While we might be tempted to answer, "Just get out of the kitchen and let me get things done.", we may wish to give pause and demonstrate a few things. The patience part of the equation also has a direct link to independence and resilience. Boys will want to watch their parents, especially a male relative barbecue, but as we all know, even while some fantastic things can be produced this way, it is only the beginning to what can be done. If you have a young man who interested in the culinary arts or just likes baking cookies, encourage his passion with opportunities, exercise patience as he will burn a few things, and give him time and space to become independent in the kitchen. Just like my grandmother, have him discover the new world that awaits him, even if it requires the perseverance required to watch a boiling pot or a simmering stew. The rewards will last a lifetime!

Bigfoot, Loch Ness, and River Monsters: Catalyst and Crucible to Engaging the Male Learner

Many may argue over the existence of Bigfoot, Loch Ness, and other fantastical concepts that scientists and, specifically, cryptzoologists, have been chasing for many years, but I divulge why it's important to engage students' minds through the discussion and study of these creatures.

"There are more things in heaven and earth, Horatio, than are dreamt of in your philosophy"—*Shakespeare, Hamlet Act 1, Scene 5*

At a recent family occasion, the always popular debate on the existence of Bigfoot arose. This is usually accompanied by similar testaments regarding the likelihood of the Loch Ness Monster, Ogopogo, the Yeti, ghosts, and of course, aliens. As a family, we have a lot of fun with this stuff relaying stories, and things we have seen in the media, all for a good laugh. However, the field of Cryptozoology, the study or pursuit of animals whose existence has not yet been proven, is a fascination for many. My students will often voice concerns that everything has been invented and discovered.

I often respond in kind with a shocked and engaging tone, relaying the fact that all of space is awaiting humanity and that according to a 2011 article in *National Geographic,* "Humans have yet to discover an astounding 86% of species on land and 91% in the oceans of the planet!" *The Adventurer* suggested that 70% of Earth is unexplored. If there was ever room for Bigfoot or Loch Ness, there it is. I truly enjoy watching young minds race when these staggering facts are placed before them. One of the greatest aspects in teaching Science at the elementary level is the omnipresence of enthusiasm, wonder, and a sense that there is still much 'magic" left in the world.

Engaging Students in Limitless Scientific Concepts outside the Classroom

These preoccupations with *the world of the fantastic* are both the catalyst and the crucible to engaging the male learner. The first unit of the Science curriculum in both the fifth and sixth grades deals with the subjects of the environment and classification. Students learn the gambit of knowledge from ecosystems to food webs, and the work of 1750's Swedish botanist Carl von Linné (who is known by the Latin form of his name, *Linnaeus*). These concepts must not sadly be relegated to the textbook alone. Teachers must engage students' minds in the laboratories of the outdoors.

Regardless of location, students and teachers can brainstorm places for these studies to commence. A favourite locale of mine has always been the Don Valley Brick Works, in Toronto. Aside from having been one of the very first ever education guides from the Todmorden Mills Museum, to conduct tours there, whilst in university; the following beguiling facts make it a winner: the appearance of fossils from pre-historic Lake Iroquois's lake bed, the terra-formed open mine now crafted into ponds and vegetation, the evidence that two ice ages occurred on the quarry rock face, and the industrial effect on the environment, brings so much more depth to the delivery of Science. Boys revel in the excitement of discovery and the tactile environments, which reinforce the text, but allow for deeper connections to take place. As much as fact is the prevailing umbrella of learning, its true support lies in the desire and imagination of its pupils, both young and old.

Nurturing and Engaging Students' Imaginations and Interests through Programming

While there is certainly a great deal of utter garbage on television and YouTube, my students will often inform me of the truly worthy programs that spark their sense of phenomenon. In keeping with our units on biodiversity and environment, one show has arisen repeatedly as being highly recommended by them: *River Monsters*. For the unfamiliar, rugged biologist Jeremy Wade travels the world for Discovery Channel looking for fish that have traversed into the realm of legend, or even having been declared extinct. A recent episode had him going after a Mongolian Taimen, a fish he had dreamt about catching even as a boy and, according to him, was a part of Chinese lore. There is an explicit link here to engaging a young male mind and inspiring him to keep that youthful sense of the unreal alive, but maturing into a serious career such as a biologist.

The following is quote from the episode guide, *"Jeremy Wade returns to Australia's croc-infested Fitzroy River for one of his toughest quests yet— to catch one of the world's rarest fish. This shark is so elusive it was only discovered ten years ago, and so rare only a handful of people have ever seen it. Almost nothing is known about this endangered beast. Could it be a man-eater?"*

What young man wouldn't be attracted to a spectacle like that? These are the type of resources that should be a part of the students' experience. A multi-layered and experiential approach to learning is required. While students will shriek and cheer for Wade's struggles, they will want to have a sense of it as well; a reason why a part of our program at Northmount is to take the boys fishing.

How to Engage Students Scientific Minds through the summer

Parents will lament that the summer recess is a brain drain of sorts, and to an extent, the critique has some merit. However, the season is an excellent time for getting out into the world with your children and discovering some of its hidden treasurers.

As an advocate of camping, I would encourage families to discover the night sky, look into the camp fire just as our ancestors did for thousands of years, try fishing and finding your own river monsters, or even listening for the elusive Bigfoot while roasting marshmallows. As a father-to-be, I am most grateful for the fact that so much geography is undiscovered, that animals and beings of an enchanted nature might still be out there, and that my boyish enthusiasm for the impossible and the improbable have reconciled themselves with the rational adult attributes of wisdom and knowledge, and not been swept under the rug of history by some misguided notion requiring me to be a starchy pillar of maturity.

I too, want to be around a camp fire with my wife and children, relaying to them the ghost stories of old Europe and the chance that monster Bigfoot is still alive in the uncharted virgin forests of North America. However, there is another part of me that wishes once and for all to silence the critics of Cryptozoology, with an announcement that might begin with, "This is CNN breaking news . . . ." Imagine that!

Sowing the Seeds of Education

Urban designers of the 19th Century had lamented the visible passing of pastoral or agricultural traditions. Many like Frederick Law Olmsted (Central Park, Mount Royal) witnessed the onslaught of the Industrial Revolution and the mass exodus from the countryside to the city. The concept of the urban park, as a respite for the physically and mentally exhausted came into vogue quickly. Even in Canada, the Fraser Institute cited that in the year 1900, about half the population still lived in the country, but by 2010, that percentage had fallen below 10%. There was arguably a cultural echo of sorts that cascaded through the 20th Century from successive generations that carried forth a community of memory from their agricultural heritage. The other significant factor was of course the continuous waves of immigration throughout the last century from Ireland, the Ukraine, and the rest of Europe through the post-world war periods, and then a further accentuation of the Canadian mosaic from all corners of the globe, in the latter half of the century. Our society has largely become an urban dwelling folk, whose perceived connection to genuine agriculture might consist of the Sunday drive, visiting a farmer's market, or for the younger, Facebook savvy crowd, playing *Farmville* over the Internet. The transition to a service and information economy has ironically left some critical and time-in-memorial expertise waning, if not forgotten. This progressive move forward has also had as a casualty boys' education.

As a child, I was always impressed with my uncle's garden. He grew a lot of flowers, which were pretty, but as a boy, I characteristically wanted some plants that delivered results: fruits and vegetables. He grew many berries, tomatoes, beans, and other produce. During the month of May, there would also be a massive pile of topsoil delivered to his home, and even though I didn't live there, on occasion, I can recall helping my cousins to cart it to the backyard. Much of the knowledge and enthusiasm for creating and maintaining a garden stuck with all of us in the family, and now as adults, we all have some sort of garden where we live. Throughout the 1980's, there still existed a significant number of Italian and Portuguese families in Scarborough. My friends from those cultures would boast huge gardens in their backyards, with tomatoes the size of one's fist, and grapes that would be pressed into wine, and then poured into the proudly displayed demijohns. Many of their traditions also reverted back to "the old country" and whether through direct instruction, or implicit inspiration, the emulation and co-opting of those skills was not lost on many from Generations X and Y. **As boys, we would ask questions, witness the results and rewards of hard work, and if lucky enough, have a parent, an uncle, or a grandfather who would transfer knowledge the old fashioned way, through experience and sweat.**

If Olmsted's parks served the tired masses of the industrial and commercial cities of the past century, then might it be fair to say that the urban garden may offer the same hiatus for the minds of the information age? Perhaps so, but our students must be afforded opportunities to learn outside of the classroom. As teachers, we need to pull them away from the complacent classroom dynamic of text-to-paper pedagogy and provide them with some real experiences. We must not fall into the trap that *Google, YouTube,* or some "app" will offer a bridge to a genuine experience supplanting a true engagement of the senses; that's bubble wrapped, lazy logic. We need to get our hands dirty again. Male students especially, need to recoup this experiential transfer of knowledge and reapply it to a personal renaissance of a love of learning.

Follow this educational paradigm and its sequence. My fifth grade class at Northmount School is reading a book entitled, *The People of Sparks* by Jeanne DuPrau, it is the sequel to the popular *The City of Ember*. Our novel depicts the struggles of the refugees of Ember and their adaptation to an agrarian culture (LANGUAGE ARTS). We are studying biodiversity, fluvial geography, and structures as individual constructs and co-existing environmental realities (SCIENCE). The Grade 5's are also learning about Mesopotamia, the Fertile Crescent, and early civilizations (SOCIAL STUDIES). During religion, we also examine the relationship between the agrarian culture of Judea in relation to the major movements regarding faith in the Old and New Testament (RELIGION). Where do we plug in the experiential learning and application?

This week we drew out a plan for a school vegetable garden, prior to which I had instructed the class on whom to call before digging. All of the respective utilities gave us the permission to commence the project. Another student recalled that the potatoes in the *City of Ember* were shriveled and weak, so we studied our desired area for total sunlight exposure. The students and I excavated a 4 meter by 9 meter plot at the back of the school. Suddenly, a rush of water seemed to explode from the side of the building. The boys all stood back in awe, and me, in fear. Had we broken a water pipe? No, it was the sump pump gushing out water from the roof and basement of the school. The boys recalled the irrigation principles they had learned about in Science and Social Studies, and decided to dig a trench that would reroute the water into the edging of the garden. Like the Babylonians and their gardens, ours too, would be almost self-sufficient as far as water was concerned. We also witnessed a rabbit and applying our biodiversity lessons and some colloquial agricultural knowledge; we placed tabasco sauce around the outside of the garden to keep vermin away. Toward the end, many of my students said they knew how hard our ancestors must have worked, how difficult the people of Ember had it in Sparks, and how good they felt about where the vegetables were going to go in September. Many deemed the experience of planting and gardening as calming and relaxing, saying as much.

Aside from cross-curricular connections, vegetable gardening also teaches empathy. Our students agreed that the produce will entirely go to one of the kitchens or organizations in the City of Toronto that takes care of the less fortunate.

Is the Future at Hand? The Case for Returning Industrial Arts to Schools

There comes a time in every rightly-constructed boy's life when he has a raging desire to go somewhere and dig for hidden treasure.
—The Adventures of Tom Sawyer, *Mark Twain*

There is something very natural about giving a boy a hammer, some wood, and nails and seeing what he can come up with. During the early 1980's, my family had the good fortune to live in a row of town houses, along sleepy Invergordon Avenue in Scarborough. The best part of that time was that behind our home were three large, over-grown apple trees and a landscape that stretched for 3 kilometers in each direction featuring only two farms, big hills, fields, and rows and rows of trees. If you go looking for this idyllic scene now you will be greeted by three separate neighbourhoods, a strip plaza, and 42 Division. However, when I was age 10 to 12, this area was perfect for high adventure and the building of forts. Most homes in the neighborhood featured working parents and kids that had as much energy as the day was long. Often, my buddies and I would be out cobbling together pieces of wood left behind by the local farmers or the construction crews that had just finished our townhomes. These mismatched materials would include old road barriers, particle board, severely knotted two-by-fours, some very thin veneers, and pieces of carpet left over from installations. To all of us, these things may have as well come directly from the lumber store, we didn't care. We built magnificent fortresses strong enough to withstand any thunderstorm, towering enough to hide from parents and babysitters, and definitely fortified enough to keep girls out! The latter surprisingly became more relaxed as we grew older. The point being was that we had educated ourselves, and each other, on the use of tools like hammers, saws, screw drivers, and when we just couldn't "eyeball it", measuring tape.

Moving further ahead to 1983 and 1984, we began taking formal shop classes. These were awesome. The directive by our teacher, the very affable and dynamic Mr. Tone, in Grade 7 was to produce something that held something else. At first we deemed the assignment boring, but then we thought about the possibilities. Several boys made skateboards, others made shelves, and some guys made record and cassette holders. Our Grade 8 year was marked by the building of swords, shields and other medieval implements. One fellow even made a very realistic looking battle axe. Mr. Tone called us the He-Man class, after the popular cartoon show. The fascinating part of the class was that it was a true equalizer of all of the different personas of the class. The athletes loved the woodworking as much as the musicians, the smart kids, and all of the rest of us. It was a Sherwood Forest of sorts, within the confines of an industrial arts shop. Everyone knew how to swing a hammer, use the different screws, and work a manual saw. We were further educated in the next step of evolution: POWER TOOLS! Learning how to use a band saw and a palm sander were just as exciting and as much of a watershed moment, as a young man earning his driver's license. All safety precautions were obviously taken, with each tool being predicated by a lecture and step-by-step instruction. Afterwards, we were free to use these tools all under the watchful eye of our teacher.

The current education system, whether it be public or private has had a significant paradigm shift away from such former staples as Industrial Arts and Auto Shop. The reasons for which include: the lack of teachers for such specialties, the shrinking budgets surrounding education, a feminization of pedagogy, and the institutional and parental impulse that most students should complete a liberal arts education, and anything less would be substandard. Also in the mix, is the inability of school administration to recognize the value of vocational education as it was not germane to their experience, culture, or academic development. Ironically, the Trades professions are the most in demand in Canada and allow for the highest importation of foreign workers into the country; which in itself, does not even satisfy the need for these skilled workers. According to Statistics Canada, *"The vast majority of workers in the trades worked full time (97% in 2007). Perhaps due to the full-time nature of most jobs in the trades, very few tradespeople held multiple jobs—only 2.5% in 2007 compared with 5.4% for other occupations."* Stats Canada also suggested that, *"Finally, the average age of those working in the trades was fewer than 40 in 2007— slightly younger than other workers (41). The aging of the population had a similar effect on both trades and non-trades—with the average age increasing by about 4 years over the past two decades. A look at the ratio of entrants (age 25 to 34) to near-retirees (50 or older) indicates that workers in the trades were in fact more in balance in 2007 than those in other occupations (1.0 versus 0.7)."* This would indicate a huge opening in positions as the aggregate age of present workers is in the forties, that massive opportunity and shortages will exist in the coming decades. The folly of those who believe everyone should have a liberal arts education lies in another myth regarding the skilled trades: they are not educated persons. Once again, Stats Canada provided contrary information, *"About 8 in 10 plumbers and electricians had postsecondary education, well above the national average. This reflects the requirements set out in the provincial certification programs."*

There is no question that the liberal arts education remains the path that we wish our children to follow. It should be noted and co-opted into our thinking, that not all students are suited for this educational stream. The problem in North America remains that alternate routes of education are still regarded as less than the "gold standard." So how then do we address the need for vocational skills for students who are clearly on the university/professional track? Two officials from differing school zones south of the border commented on the issue. *"We are not getting teachers in the pipeline with majors in Industrial Arts,"* Profitt said. The ABC district is not alone. *Shop classes—the wood, drafting, print, metal and other industrial arts courses that **served as a rite of passage for generations of men**—are fast disappearing from the curricula of junior and senior high schools. "There is still a need for the skills taught in Industrial Arts courses, **especially for our academically oriented students.** Any person who owns a home should be able to repair a molding, fix an electrical plug or refinish a piece of furniture,"* said Terence Garner, assistant superintendent of personnel for Dade County Public Schools.

Northmount's recent Go-Kart club highlighted the need for some Industrial Arts skills to be made a part of the informal/

extra-curricular curriculum. Most boys, if asked, would say Philips, Frearson, and Robertson were probably hockey players. They are not, those are all screwdriver types. Our students took great delight in learning how to properly swing a hammer, sink a nail, cut wood, and fashion a dock for the go-kart. The look on their faces and the numerous comments reflecting the joy of the moment resounded in statements like, "Is this great or what?" The grade eight students actually visited a shop, not only learning how to make a long board, but assisting in the construction of them. While we have always had an element of woodworking and shop in our Fine Arts classes and clubs, Northmount's 2012 Gala will supply the school with some much needed hand and power tools for the students so as to increase this much needed competency and desired masculine experience. Perhaps for our era, the treasure that Mr. Twain speaks of rests in the hands of the students who will fashion their own adventures and fortunes from the skills, both academic and proficient, they learned as developing young men. If fortune favours the bold, then the expedition of the future is in the minds and hands of our students.

Science Fiction Casts a Light from the Future to the Present and Back Again

Whether it was H.G. Wells taking us on a ride in *The Time Machine* or Isaac Asimov unveiling the secrets of robotics in *I Robot*, children have always been fascinated with science fiction. It is a literary source which truly lends itself to all sorts of media incarnations from television to the silver screen. Science fiction has become the heir apparent to the nursery rhyme or children's story. The genre asks us to reach beyond the possible and suspend our belief when we delve into a new world that has some surprisingly conventional and moral messages. These tales of the future are particularly poignant with male readers as they contain some of the bastions of successful boy-centered literacy: action, a definable antagonist and protagonist, mystery, a struggle, new inventions, aliens or monsters, and hope for an exciting future. Above all, science fiction might be the key to our own future. Perhaps there exists a direct correlation, a type of paradox, between the decline of male literacy and that of innovation and original ideas? As an example, at one time there were 220 manufacturers of television sets in North America, there are now only 24.1

"The N.A.A.L. (National Assessment of Adult Literacy) administered tests which revealed that an estimated 14% of US residents would have extreme difficulty with reading and written comprehension. These people can legally be defined as illiterate. This could lead to numerous problems for these people now and in the future".2

As we slide further into becoming a consumer driven economy, the aspirations for a more lofty future rests in the minds of our students who may forge an alternative economic paradigm based on a patent driven, knowledge-based, information economy. While we won't manufacture very much in the future, perhaps this might be replaced with the production of ideas and technological breakthroughs in the fields of Science, Engineering, Robotics, Communications, Information Technology, Medicine, and other such domains. The creative drives for these innovations are first inspired by connections that are made by children through experience, media, and literacy. Gene Roddenberry, the creator of Star Trek, often remarked that the technology only dreamt of in his series came to fruition within decades of their presentation as fictional gizmos of the future. While the "experts" predicted flying cars and personalized jet packs, Roddenberry's Star Trek ushered into existence such things as the cell phone, lap top computers, microwaves, lasers, and the big screen monitor (the real reason everyone wanted to take over the Enterprise). There was most certainly a direct correlation between written science fiction and its propensity to inspire young minds in the fields of engineering and design. It appears as if each successive generation could be inspired by some vision of the future.

Although it was presented as occurring "A Long Time Ago, In a Galaxy Far, Far Away", Star Wars captivated three successive generations and counting, with an alternate vision of the future. George Lucas' stunning, six-part saga placed the innovation bar into the stratosphere. The assumptions of these movies included the yet to be designed light saber, faster-than-light hyperspace, advanced artificial intelligence, and an answer to the ever elusive are we alone question, that it seemed by Star Wars' reality, a common place status quo. A fascinating dichotomy exits within these films and books that are quite striking. Even though the technology was so far advanced, it is all held together by ancient, yet most relevant truths regarding the active role of good and evil. One of its central morals was that while technology may be extraordinarily advanced, basic spiritual notions unique to the core of the soul are tangible and relevant regardless of the setting. The phrase, "May the force be with you, and also with you," is as sincere on an inter-galactic spaceship as its religious counterpart. Thus, one can forge great scientific strides without abandoning what is true and eternal to existence. This variant of truth will ultimately veer humanity toward destruction or utopia. George Lucas once said, "Whatever has happened in my quest for innovation has been part of my quest for immaculate reality." This is in essence the nature of the hermeneutic circle of meaning behind science fiction and real-time innovation.

If we stop reading and connecting, the quest for "the perfect world" will increasingly cease to exist in increments of chronological time. It is not ever possible to attain a complete utopia. However, should we freeze in our ability to dream, design, and delve into the future; we too, will lose opportunities for immaculate realities to manifest themselves in brief epochs of time. It is encouraging to see students reading the classic narratives and new ones with a gleam in their eye that surely marries the concepts of science, literacy, and faith. Science fiction passes the torch of innovation to a new generation of eager minds who will undoubtedly light an inspirational path from what could be, to what is.

http://www.tvhistory.tv/1960-2000-TVManufacturers.htm, cited October 17, 2011.
http://www.caliteracy.org/rates, cited October 17, 2011.

Where is Our Albert Einstein?

Take a look at the world in 2014, it's aching; job losses continue to climb, consumer confidence is low, and fears of a depression are no longer the stuff of political commentators, but part of lunch room conversation. Do you ever wonder why the price of a DVD player is easily under $100 or why one can acquire a fairly decent computer for under $300? The reason is that we have ceased being innovators and have largely become consumers. Youth and I dare say many adults have adopted a mind set based solely on acquisition without effort. Our technology is outdated and only improved by software design and memory modifications. We, like Sir Isaac Newton, are "standing on the shoulders of giants" but unlike Newton, we are about to fall off.

There is hope and it's not in any government bailout or restructuring program; it's in our youth and in the Science Fairs that should be going on in all schools. These are unique vehicles that allow for the purest expression of innovation to occur. I am not suggesting that anyone is going to even the next great product, but you never know? Children are naturally inquisitive and are full of wonder especially in such a dynamic field as Science. Just ask the folks down at the Ontario Science Centre or which top grossing films of all time are Science related. 13 of 30 are. In fact one, Jurassic Park, even contains Science lessons.

The Ontario Curriculum's Science and Technology sections 2.1 to 2.7, openly call for "developing investigation and communications skills." From building models to circuits and the conducting of experiments with proper scientific notation and process; the province's design for

Science and learning is sound. |Boards and their constituent schools should re-examine the restoration of competitive Science Fairs with some adjustments for self-esteem and younger students. Competition is an aspect of learning some educators have shied away from. However, for boys, this could not have been a worse decision. If young men feel nothing is at stake, then their sense of effort and innovation will decline. Junior school students, from SK to Grade 3, should be encouraged to simply present a project and become accustomed to communicating their ideas to others. The intermediate to senior students can be grouped into comparative groups with awards for 1st, 2nd, 3rd, and honourable mention as well as an award for creativity and innovation. It is truly remarkable as to what can appear if students believe it matters and it will distinguish them amongst their peers. One need only examine the rise in robotic competitions and kit sales. This is real competition, not the artificial gimmick found in video games.

Teachers will often tell you that they have seem some truly beautiful, outstanding, and utterly creative projects submitted by students, but done by parents. It is at this point where two of the most contentious issues of the Science Fair can be dealt with: the last minute surprise, which usually begins with, "Mom, guess what Monday is?" And the authorship question. If educators reconstruct the Science Fair into small phases and have the students do the entire project during class time, the fair will truly become equitable, the tension on the home front will diminish considerably, and students will use their own imagination and abilities to create a project, which can truly be assessed for learning. Schools will discover that far more parents will be interested in attending the Science Fair, students will be enthusiastic, and the cliché projects of the volcano, the lemon generator, and the household cleaner comparisons will fade into memory-maybe. Tim O'Reilly president of O'Reilly Media recently commented that persons of our time are asking themselves two significant questions: Where is our Albert Einstein? Why are we not working on the researching the real stuff? Start looking at your local Science Fair.

What is the Problem with Mathematics Today?

If we were to think about what consists of a classic education: reading, writing, and mathematics, we might reflect upon our own educational histories and best view these three pillars as separate, but equal. Educational psychologists will assert that two of these factors (reading and writing) are grounded in left brain activity, while mathematics is grounded in the right brain. This has always assisted students who were more inclined toward operating in a given sphere of the mind. To extrapolate the argument further, the majority of male students operate from that very section. However, the two solitudes of language arts and mathematics have experienced a higher than normal convergence during the last couple of decades. Of course, mathematics always had some degree of language integration in the form of decoding questions and arriving at a result from the analysis of a word problem. That was fair game. Math students knew that questions would not always be presented in pure numerical fashion, and word problems existed to challenge them and integrate some "real life" scenarios into the program. Their teachers knew that some math competencies required language such as ratio, per cent, problems, and time. Some of our parents' generation had trouble in understanding what was known as the "new math" and could aid us only to a certain level. The problem today is that the new math has become "new and improved" (to borrow a trendy tagline), and now both parents and students are caught in a system that values less accuracy, places little emphasis on basic fundamentals, and seeks to explore reasoning, rather than results.

Most of the mathematics programs that are being delivered in Ontario are faulty. Examine the following EQAO results from Grade Six: 2005 (60%); 2006 (61%); 2007 (59%); 2008 (61%); and 2009 (63%). The per-cent results indicated how many students across Ontario were meeting provincial standards. Boys are generally performing 2-4% worse than girls, in a field they once dominated. In terms of gender, all of our students need to be doing much better! So what is wrong? Let us begin with an examination of the structure of the textbook itself. Math texts are generally divided into self-contained units. Students know that if they are not good at geometry or fractions, they can "run out the clock" and not see these units until the following grade. There is little or no building of competencies across a wider length of time, a critical tenet in producing unshakeable foundation from which a future math scholar might be forged. If textbooks were to be reorganized into short lessons that introduce new concepts, while continuously revisiting past skill sets, this incremental approach would produce highly skilled students. Thus, what has been taught in Lesson 14 will still have representation in Lesson 135. Discover the research surrounding Saxon Math and Singapore Math, two non-units, incrementally based systems, and their ability to fashion students who retain a great deal more knowledge at the conclusion of the school year.

Many of the Math textbooks used in Ontario are too colourful and look like magazines. They ask questions that are deemed, by many students, as unnecessary and frivolous. It is without question that the process of how an answer is achieved must be evaluated and part of student learning. However, the essence of mathematics and its attraction to it, by students, is the nature of its pure right and wrong clarity. Using elaborate language to explain how an answer was arrived at, but not knowing the basic functional skills to achieve the answer, is a waste of time. Teachers need to evaluate the "showing of work" through calculation, which employs methods/formulas. They do not need to ask students how they felt about the problem or how to formulate in words basic mathematical processes. The ironic tragedy, regarding elementary and middle-school mathematics is that, once students enter secondary school, many of these core skills they will need to succeed are either are absent, or severely lacking. Secondary level education assumes that basic competencies are known to the students, and that they are capable of solving the two-to-four-step solutions with some degree of automatic competency. They do not have the time to draw diagrams and work with manipulatives in the ninth grade, while offering their insights in journals into their feelings and motivations arriving at a numerical answer.

Parents should take note from the best practices of the tutoring centres in Toronto. They should begin the process by having their children learn their times tables cold: no figures, no manipulatives, and straight old school rote memory. It might be a tough battle, but the skill set will last them a lifetime. You and your children must discover what they can and cannot do by reviewing their textbook. Turn to each page, and simply perform a yes or no diagnostic. Upon completion of this process, create a top-ten list, and work through each skill set over a timetable that is appropriate for the family's particular set of circumstances. The sobering conclusion is that the textbook is not the whole story. There are some excellent publications that narrow in on specific skills, and through clear explanations and repeated practice (frequency of examples is greater), you can cross them off your list. It has been my experience, that if there is a partnership between the home and the school, and a recognition that one can share in the work of the other, together they can achieve success. Mathematics is akin to basic life skills and higher intelligence. Bloom's Taxonomy suggests a foundation is required to reach the ability to analyze, synthesize, and evaluate. The major disconnect with mathematics in elementary school and, subsequently, in secondary school, appears to be the nature and quality of the foundational intelligences required to reach up to the upper echelons of achievement.

MINDing Our Words

During a recent Grade 3 Language Arts class, a spelling/vocabulary word of little note appeared on the dictation and usage list. The word was *mental*. It was defined as, having to do with the mind, a mental activity was not a physical one, and Chess was given as a real-life example. I would have thought this to be rather innocuous, and at best, a trivial moment in the day's affairs. As is often the case, what was deemed to be insignificant by an adult was not always so in the mind of a third grade student who has other ideas. Quite innocently, one of my students raised his hand and stated, "Sir, there is a boy at my swimming class who's mental." Not to be out done, another student chimed in and announced that, "There's this man where I go shopping who is quite mental and yells things." Full stop, (to borrow an over-used term) a teachable moment the size of a Mack truck had descended up-on all of us in the third grade. I quickly halted the dictation and explained that the boy at the swimming class is probably Mentally Challenged and the man at the shopping centre was unfortunately mentally ill. A pause shrouded the room, but my explanation had switched on the levers of the eager young brains before me; I could tell because half of them looked in the air and everyone's eyes, including mine, were shifting back and forth. The pensive silence was broken by another student, who, having heard all of the aforementioned semantics, came to this conclusion: "Sir, I am not great in Math; I think I am Mentally Challenged." Oh boy!

I often think that one of the reasons I have enjoyed teaching boys for some thirteen years, with some measure of success, is derived from a Germanic cultural attribute of being clear in one's tone and intent, and not couching language in ambiguous niceties. Naturally, one needs to weave in a measure of Canadian diplomacy and sensitivity especially in an elementary school setting. However, the level of this "so called" couched language in ambiguous niceties has morphed out of its agreeable tenet found in the social graces into language that is in itself per-flexing and defeatist to whom it is supposedly helping or defining without insult—political correctness run amuck. To borrow from a true observer of Western cultural discourse, comedian George Carlin (1937-2008) lamented the issue of mental illness in regards to soldiers.

"In the first World War, that condition was called 'Shell Shock.' Simple, honest, direct language. Two syllables. Shell Shock. Almost sounds like the guns themselves. That was seventy years ago. Then a whole generation went by, and the Second World War came along. And the very same combat condition was called 'Battle Fatigue.' Four syllables now. Takes a little longer to say, doesn't seem to hurt as much. 'Fatigue' is a nicer word than 'shock.' Then we had the war in Korea in 1950. The very same combat condition was called 'Operational Exhaustion.' And the humanity has been completely squeezed out of the phrase, it's totally sterile now. Operational Exhaustion, sounds like something that might happen to your car! Then, of course, came the war in Vietnam, the very same condition was called 'Post-traumatic Stress Disorder.' Still eight syllables, but we've added a hyphen! And the pain is completely buried under jargon. 'Post-traumatic Stress Disorder.' I'll bet you if we'd have still been calling it Shell Shock, some of those Vietnam veterans might have gotten the attention they needed at the time. I'll bet you that."—**George Carlin**

Back to Grade 3, innocence and curiosity demands an answer. Unlike, Carlin's observation of Shell Shock, the language surrounding those whom we now refer to as *Mentally Challenged* has had a rather

123

unfortunate and disingenuous past. Early 20th Century words (*Morons, Imbeciles,* and *Idiots*) for those with an Intelligent Quotient (I.Q.) under 70 have devolved into modern insults. They were replaced with the term *Mental Retardation.* The American Association of Intellectual and Developmental Disabilities posits, "The term *Intellectual Disability* covers the same population of individuals who were diagnosed previously with *Mental Retardation.*" Depending on where one resides in the English speaking world the two terms, *Mentally Challenged* or *Intellectual Disability,* hold sway in polite language. The inherent difficulty, as seen in Grade 3, is that the term is ambiguous and can devolve into less than appropriate language. While *mental* doesn't quite have the same sting as perhaps those early 20th Century design-nations, the short form of the 1970's identification of *Mental Retardation (Retard),* surely does. The unfortunate paradox is that its replacement terms in polite language often fail to make the correct connection to this disability. So what does a parent or teacher do with this controversial issue in language? Address it. Depending on the maturity of the class or individual, the following can be done:

1) Correct the student gently and inform them of the proper language. Don't stop there. Most will.
2) Make it clear that the words *Mental* and *Retard* are short forms of medical terms that have become insults.
3) Most importantly, relate to them that the use of those words actually go far beyond that of an insult and hurt all Mentally Challenged people, their opportunities in life, and their devoted families.
4) I often relay to them personal stories of interaction with Mentally Challenged persons in my life.

By elementary school, and likely before, children learn that words are powerful and can wound others. They have a personal responsibility in how they wield them. Recently, a voracious reader in the fifth grade approached me with the work of Mark Twain. While I did not have the time to review his text and see if it indeed contained the racial epitaphs we now so view as vulgar and offensive, the book appeared as if it was in its original language written in Missouri of the 19th Century. While I will not repeat the word in question here, as I believe it has descended to the moral depths and depravities of English vulgarity, I did in fact inform him of the word in question, its etymology (derived from the word ignorant) and its severe impact on persons who might be affected by its utterance, which in fact, should be us all! It was predicated that while it was indeed tremendous literature, it was written in an era with faults and failings, and a lexicon which has now fallen out of favour in polite society. Mr. Domina (Headmaster), who appeared at the impromptu meeting fascinatingly and wisely, suggested that, "There are words and phrases we may use in daily communication and written text today, that in one hundred years might be deemed highly offensive, yet we have no indication that in 2013, that might be so."

Education is knowledge, and its genuine and moral application is wisdom. Words shape the actions of others and us. They can elicit fear, prejudice, and anger; they can also usher in change, empathy and understanding. Words can also heal. While enrolled in my undergrad program, I had the pleasure of giving tours at Todmorden Mills Museum in the Don Valley. A disinterested high school class came through near the end of June. My colleague gave them a tour. Integrated into this trip was a mentally challenged young man. I offered to take him around as he was most interested in everything we had. I spent two hours talking about artefacts and answering all his questions. At the end of the tour, the rest of the class was primed to leave. However, this young man introduced me to his father and said, "This has been the best day of my life." He paused, looked at me and stated, "You should be-come a teacher." Herein lays the link from the lexicon to life. Were we to discount persons because of malicious or misunderstood words, we might, as author Steven Pinker (in another context) relates, "Miss out on the better angels of our nature."

Classroom Collisions:
Elementary School Children on
the Wrong Side of History

The way of the world has a unique manner in which it enters a school and classroom. Children are sensitive to the affairs of society and culture. They are not oblivious to the larger events to which their parents and older siblings to and which they discuss. Students will ask questions, debate, formulate exaggerations and opinions. Elementary school children will also begin to form a sense of temporal history in relation to who they are as individuals and how they fit into the grand scheme of culture and time. The notion of self-discovery is both an internal and external dynamic. It operates through an ongoing reciprocating paradigm that grows with maturity and ability to inference meaning from external influences that are ultimately reconciled and given validity in the child's mind. Children feel the *spirit of the age* and its relationship to them.

While they may not be able to explain and surmise the deep questions and challenges of an era in which they exist, children do have a sense of the major developments of a period and the importance given to them through explicit images and the process of formulation and retelling. As an example, the 1980's were a time of nuclear angst and a positioning of the world in two camps. Young students excel at comparison and they value judgments. In essence, they would ask who the "good guys" and the "bad guys" were. Depending on their culture, and how the world is framed for them by home and school, they would arrive at an answer. This is a critical insight into the thought processes of an elementary school child. There is a significant tenet missing in this equation: analysis and synthesis. An ability to identify, discerns, and reconciles the "grey areas" of meaning and interpretations are not part of a child's cognitive process; they are guided by their own connection of meaning through the framing of faith, culture, society and education.

Teachers will tell you that true learning is taking place when a child can retain knowledge over a long period of time by attaching what has been learned to experience and memory. Learning, unlike the linear progression of the school year and worldly events, occurs in a metaphysical paradigm that ebbs and flows in the mind of the child from the past to the present and the future, adding context and significance. It is knowledge becoming wisdom being modified by experience and constantly reapplied and reorganized. At this point, a symbiosis of the knowledge is connected to an aspect of their emotions and experiences. This becomes problematic when an issue, already framed by media and society, enters the realm of classroom. The simple dynamic chosen by children to discern their own meaning on a given topic becomes skewed when they have some identification with a group that society has deemed "the other" or, perhaps even worse, "the enemy". For many educators, this may or may not be a new factor in the classroom. Certainly, Canadian History tells us during the Pre-Confederation and Post-Confederation eras, Canada welcomed people representing nations Canadians had fought against in either an ideological or direct manner. This speaks to the tolerance, acceptance, and the greatness of Canada. This Canadian attitude has shaped the world view of many of its students through the ages.

The sheer growth of Canada's diversity through multiculturalism makes the aforementioned process quite relevant. A text-based approach to learning the history of this country is a good start, but relying solely on text and pen-to-paper assignments and evaluations is insufficient. Teachers must always be cognisant of potential collision situations. The instruction of history, modern or ancient, can be fraught with peril for the teacher. History can be an emotionally difficult subject for children because of the following factors:

Nationalities retain the same names and countries. (Identification)

The echo of history is much louder for those children who are closer to recent events and have relatives that have participated in conflict-ridden times.

The proximity to actual experience varies in the classroom. Students may have direct involvement or salient memories of events.

In multi-generational families, old attitudes and prejudice colour the objectivity of the student and introduce a toxic dynamic that the culture of the home, while legitimately preferred, is also far superior to others. (Ranking)

The power of the eyewitness account supersedes text. A child or a family member might have `been there`` and will contradict the `big picture`` analysis found in course books.

Aside from a direct censorship of history and current events, can teachers avoid classroom collisions? Not really. Educators can utilize a set of mechanisms in order to "keep the peace" and present an equitable portrayal of events: historical and current. We must avoid the scourge of politically correct language because of its emptiness of spirit and numbing of truth, which does history and its students no measurable good. A discussion on the nature of truth and the selection of facts as a means to writing history are excellent beginnings. If children can observe how history is written, their understanding of its presentation in oral or written form will provide them with one of their first critical tools in understanding. It is obvious that the teacher must couch any personal bias or opinions on a historical matter in order to preserve the purity of the teaching. If teachers do engage in personal opinion, it is their professional and moral obligation to clearly indicate the moment that they speak with the voice of opinion, rather than that of teacher. As an example, if students know a teacher is an Afghan, they will enquire as to that person's opinion on the situation in Afghanistan. The quality of the response from the teacher will dictate the behavioural expectations on any other personal intersections with history and current events in that classroom.

The mechanisms that would achieve a desired neutral investigation of history would include the following:

Pre-emptive Measures

Celebrate the distinctive cultures of the class. Have the students choose a grandparent from their family and create a project that honours him/her. Bring in food from the various ethnicities, and share.

We all are Canadians

While countries will be discussed, and some students will identify themselves with those nations, distinguish the role of the regime vs. the individual. Always make the case for Canada. "We all are Canadians, and this is a nation of immigrants." This creates a natural equality and also reflects the uniqueness of the First Nations people. Give numerous examples of conflicted groups who are able to live and work side by side in Canada, regardless of what may be happening elsewhere. A central theme of Canadian society is this remarkable ability of its people.

Recognize Injustice through Universal Truths

Religious-based schools might have an easier time with this, because they would have an existing doctrine, like the Ten Commandments, to define boundaries and laws. However, the influx of character education to mould the culture of schools would suffice. Both approaches generate empathy.

Recognize the Role of the Individual

Racism and other forms of social injustice and aggression come from the creation of people as "the other" and the fear of them. Teach that personal connections lift the veil of fear and ignorance. Suggest that while the students may be of a particular ethnicity, they themselves had nothing to do with the genesis or prosecution of a historical injustice.

Introduce the Idea of Unfair Comment

Classroom rules should always be displayed, but certainly spoken of frequently and enforced. Rules regarding the use of slurs and putdowns relating to things a person cannot change, such as their culture, ethnicity, traditions, and faith, are deemed unfair comments.

Create Your Own Iconography

It is no secret that nations unify their people by creating myths, legends, and symbols that every citizen can identify with. All of your students belong to the school and to your class. The school team logo is a good start.

The Personal Touch

Observe the tone of the lessons that might touch off a collision. Present both or multiple sides in a manner that is neutral and perceived as fair.

Talk and listen to your students. Ask the questions that you know your students may not want to broach. Referee, if a conflict occurs, and do not hesitate to involve the parents: first, through communication, then, if necessary, set up a group to resolve the issue.

The Universality of "The Villain"

Every ethnic, cultural, or national group has at least one villain. And, sometimes one is all that is needed to turn history into a violent blood bath. The purpose of this mechanism is to have the conflicted parties look into their collective mirror and decide that their background is as imperfect as the next person's. This exercise will demonstrate the futility in painting one group with the same brush stroke. All Italians are not in the Mafia, and all Germans are not Nazis, are two such examples.

To deny that emotion and learning are separate from each other is folly, and makes the case for the use of political correctness. Teachers and schools undertake every effort to encourage belonging. History, whether it is current or ancient, can be mishandled or misinterpreted, and result in severe classroom collisions, because it is inextricably bound to culture, ethnicity, and religion. Unlike any other discipline taught, history's conflicts can leap off the page and cause havoc for the teacher who has underestimated its power or failed to realize the impact on students who have a connection to the content depicted. Can collisions over history be eliminated? No, but they can be tempered to a fair academic discussion, if the aforementioned mechanisms are utilized. If History is truly the crucible of how we define ourselves as a people, then our teachers must ensure that the explosiveness of the elements have been concentrated enough to spark intelligent debate, rather than conflict.

A Formula for Success:
Does your I.Q. match your E.Q.?

There are five factors which will ultimately determine the experience of a child as they go through their formative educational years. These major factors include the following: interested and engaged parent(s) who possess a moral compass, a work ethic modeled and reinforced by the family, an I.Q. bolstered by an engaging and dynamic curriculum, emotional stability, and good mental health. The latter two factors form the E.Q., or emotional quotient. It plays a critical role in the development of the child's psychological and emotional state of well-being. The E.Q. can, like the other three counterparts, of the "*functional five*" derail a student's development and hinder their growth through school. You have probably noticed that I have not used the words achievement, career, or university. Those modifiers of achievement are unique to each person and defined as such by the individual, their family, and society; sometimes in harmony, and in other cases, in opposition.

York University and its Faculty of Education recently presented a lecture by Dr. Kwame McKenzie, who is a Senior Scientist within the Social Equity and Health Research section, the Deputy Director of Continuing & Community Care in the Schizophrenia Program, a Professor in the Department of Psychiatry at the University of Toronto, and a Professor at the Institute of Philosophy Diversity and Mental Health, University of Lancashire (England). Dr. McKenzie noted that, "The production of Social Capital which shapes a community is linked to a variety of factors, two of which, Bonding and Bridging, are most important." It was posited that, "Social Capital is the process that shapes our communities through norms, trust, and shared goals and that Bonding in the family unit (nuclear and extended) is the primary E.Q., but Bridging, the process of making connections through external relationships is the pivotal factor in nurturing good mental health." The correlation to character education and to student guidance is striking.

A current theme of discourse in the media is the quasi-war or protracted conflict between the expectations of the parent community versus that of their children's teachers; both sides accusing the other of acquiescing their responsibilities and placing the onus of child rearing and education upon the other. As this paradigm shifts continually from the realm of the verbal taunt to the manifestation of open dissatisfaction and disharmony between these two stakeholder groups, the primary concern, the student, is either left in a perpetual limbo, or worse, learns to manipulate both polar opposites to their advantage. Schools like Northmount, that have broken this artificial and dysfunctional relationship have greatly benefitted. When the expectations and goals of the home and the school are mirrored, reinforced, and forged in an active and living partnership for the benefit of the student, then the concepts of Bonding and Bridging are drawn closer together, perhaps in a type of symbiotic psychological synthesis that was previously thought to be unattainable. In essence, the emotional depth of bonding within the family structure might be replicated to bridging relationships outside of the family; a very powerful booster of mental health. I believe this is why Northmount's one-to-one Advisory Program reaps such benefits.

"Show me your friends and I will tell you who you are." This well-known phrase has passed through many homes and down through time. However, it has much deeper implications than the mirroring effect of behavior on peer groups and friends. It also speaks to the ability of a child to independently make lasting connections to their community and gain their own sense of Social Capital and thusly, good mental health. Placing students in an environment where this is not left to happenstance and their own child's sense of social intelligence, likeability, and charisma is a proactive step toward assisting the fashioning of sound mental health. A school that fosters and engages virtues that relate to the forging, maintaining, and growing of healthy, positive, and virtuous friend-ships places its entire student constituency on a defined path toward future success. While the school cannot make other children become your child's friend, it can enlarge the meaning and parameters of friendship and more importantly, the social functions of companionship and empathy. This is much like growing a bean plant. Of course, the hearty bean will generally sprout and begin to grow, but given the right location, sunlight, food, water, and soil, a robust and fruit bearing plant will emerge. If the aspects of bonding are brought closer to the school experience and perhaps even co-opted by it through authentic parent partnerships, then too, bridging activities can be guided by the school with the real belief that these bridging connections are independent of the partnership might want and yield.

The polite society and warmth of community, which we all want for our schools and for the experience of our children is within our grasp, and in some schools like Northmount, within our midst. As much as we educate our children, it is the community that also must become knowledgeable of these functions of social capital and good mental health. School communities that have created this paradigm will have an atmosphere rich in empathy, the social flexibility to deal with controversial issues based on the morality of the school community, and tackle issues of parent/student concern rapidly, avoiding high frequency, long duration, incidents of bullying and aggression. A healthy school community has as its pinnacle of success, the future of the student as a person of character and wisdom, who has been looked after by all concerned and pointed toward a brilliant path with five critical factors to light their way.

Part Three

—Notions of Time and Place in 21st Century Education—

The German International School of Toronto:
Why to Immerse a Child in a 21st Century Education, Driven by the German International School of Toronto

Parents whose children are now at the point of time of entering elementary school are faced with a myriad of choices and educational philosophies. Families also quickly begin to realize that a 21st Century education is markedly different than their own experience. The 21st Century will unfold as an international century. Will a child have the necessary framework and learning competencies to be successful both on a domestic and international level? Consider the paradigm of a German international education in Canada. The German educational approach evolves into an international satellite because, while other cultural interpretations of it will utilize it to their ends, students will have at the core of their development an infrastructure, which is wholly transferable to any nation across the planet. Explore why a German education, based in Canada can offer a child a brilliant future.

Why to Immerse a Child in a 21st Century Education, Driven by the German International School of Toronto

The concept of an immersion-type education is quite familiar to Canadians. The model that we are perhaps most acquainted with is, of course, French. However, there is another distinctive paradigm that Canadians would find quite intriguing. As the global community continues to become more of an inter-linked construct, notions of progressive education are in flux. The mere mention of the word connection in its current form, fosters brave new visions of education that break the bonds of curricular restriction and subject specific criteria for learning. Children and adolescents are now seeing themselves as part of a bigger picture. National boundaries and the limitations of geography, have given rise to new notions and perceptions of physical and temporal space. The world of the 21st Century will operate in three distinct conceptual/perceptual spheres: the physical plain, temporal limitations, and the virtual world. The one constant in all of these expressions of reality is the mastery of languages and the conception and implementation of an education that is perhaps best suited for a malleable future. This "undiscovered country", the future, will be best served by persons who cannot only communicate in the languages of the world, but have the ability to convey culture and its virtues through encounters in academia, business, and the arts. To be grounded in the reality of only one nation's educational system, would be to essentially ignore the world of promise and potential prosperity in an international setting.

Thus, the question arises: Is there an educational approach that not only delivers the precepts of excellence of its host community, but also possesses the framework of the new international century and vision to create a duality of achievement in both a domestic and global market place? The short answer is, yes. However, comprehending this unique hybrid does require some examination. In order to fully surmise the implementation of a German pedagogy in a Canadian context, some presuppositions and perceptions of the German educational system need to be dispelled. While the ethos, approach, methods and means remain the hallmarks of a German education, its supplantation into a

Canadian environment has not occurred without some symbiosis of the host's realities in which it has been placed e.g., schools in Germany generally function by way of a much earlier start. While Germans might prefer this timing, the Canadian cultural standard for a school day would run contrary to that, thus the German schools in Canada modify this time accordingly. Time may appear to be a trivial factor for many, but in a German mindset, it has much to do with cultural perceptions of orderliness.

Prospective families might perform some initial research, examining exactly what a German education involves, but come across the often startling reality that the German system has a much earlier streaming strategy than that of Canada. This strategy is in regards to the separation of students by the way of ability. This is differentiation is a rigid means of intellectual and cognitive selection and not differentiation as a teaching method to support children in the classroom. To further clarify, this division of students takes place around the end of the fourth grade, in Germany. The grade classification is the same in Canada and in Germany. Grades Five and Six are considered "Orientierungsstufe" (the orientation stage) in most German states/provinces, but the reality is that the separation still takes effect at the end of grade 4 as this is the official end of "Grundschule"— end of primary Grades One to Four.

While Canadian schools offer mainly sound liberal arts and science curriculums with accommodations and ultimately a division of streams by secondary school with some opportunities to switch differentiated levels, the German system is more defined and rigid in its separation of students by way of ability around what would be our sixth grade. However, prospective parents need not concern themselves with this guiding principle in Canada. The German International School of Toronto does not engage in any sort of differentiation strategy. Rather its symbiosis of the curriculum of Thuringia (A state in the German Federal Republic) and the Ontario Program of Studies delivers a robust pedagogy featuring the best aspects of both systems. An advantage to this hybrid education is the ability to provide individualized teaching, because the class sizes are very small. The combination of both systems suits both ex-pat students and domestic ones. The German International School of Toronto posits great success in the re-integration of its students whose families may choose to return to Germany, and with families who remain in Canada, or are based in Canada, who ultimately reintegrate back into the domestic educational system with much success. Take, for instance, the German International School's good rating in the EQAO testing. According to Principal Arnd Rupp, "The German students do very well considering the fact that some of them have just been to Canada for a year or one-and-a-half years. These students do often achieve at least provincial standard in one or two of the three assessment areas but there are also students who achieve a "reaches provincial standard". For someone who has just recently moved to Canada, and taking part in a national English exam with English not as his or her mother tongue these results are quite remarkable."

Thus, the concern over permanent displacement due to some early stratification of ability is unwarranted. In fact, the litmus test for the school's ultimate success is proven by the performance of its students in Canada and Germany. Immersion education can become problematic if this reintegration into the home land of the language or that of the host country becomes turbulent. This is simply not the case with this particular immersion approach.

The hybridization of the Thuringia and Ontario curriculums fosters an innovative methodology that when scrutinized offers some truly unique insights into what precisely a German international education looks like and how it functions for the best interests of its constituent families. This is clearly an element that needs to be understood and communicated to all potential enquiring parents. They would be intrigued by the fact that the German International School of Toronto does a lot of Cooperative Learning by Norman Green who is a Canadian citizen (he used to live in the Durham region). His learning approach of cooperative learning strategies and individualization is highly recognized and appreciated in Germany. One of the precepts of the 21st Century in regards to the educational experience of its children will be the evaluation of core and add value propositions in education. Thus, in order to understand what a German international education, (based in Canada) would mean, would be to comprehend the virtues and values of the culture itself. Education is not a cultural vacuum; it takes its value propositions from the culture(s) from out of which it is born out of, exists within, and is mirrored in the home. German values and virtues as defined by the culture become a natural extension of the delivery of its educational methods and principles. Virtues like industriousness, respect, perseverance, humility, and integrity are woven into the fabric of the environment of the school. These universal virtues are disseminated through the German framework of cultural transmission and become part of the ethos and traits that enhance the methods and means of learning offered by the German system ensconced in Canada. What then can be said of the conveyance of content and the key differentiating factors of this educational experience?

The German educational model in its Canadian setting is not a content-driven archetype in language mastery per se, but something far more intricate and exceptional. If one were to use the analogy of an iceberg, its content would be at the top. However, that content is in many respects cursory. It is benchmarked and finds its source material in the hybridization of the aforementioned curricula, but it is the massive underpinnings of the approach to this content that gets at the heart of this immersion model. Content is traditionally something that is covered by a teacher, demonstrated, experimented, and then, with the use of some assessment tool like a test or presentation, it is confirmed that the content has been understood and applied by the students. While this is certainly part of what occurs in the classrooms of the German International School of Toronto, it is does not reflect the realities of the entire picture and methodology. The add value proposition for students is that the German educational approach rests content upon technique and foundations of learning. Thus, content is analogous to placing a top hat on a well-dressed individual.

The foundations of a German international education rest in the supporting precepts of its ideology. These precepts, regardless of the influence of the host nation, remain largely intact and unmodified. Below content rests reasoning and rhetoric. The ability to deconstruct content, make inferences and connections, and then extrapolate new criticisms and ideas from the content is a much lauded competency that certainly utilizes the virtues of humility and creative perseverance. It is a manifestation of what perhaps can be regarded as the much valued trait of thoroughness. In order to examine the basis and positioning of content, the incorporation and deliberate instruction of analysis, inference, and synthesis rest in all aspects of the delivery of curriculum-based content. Students learn the world behind the text and information, and discover through textual reverse engineering how content came to be, how it can be applied and, most importantly, how it can be remodeled to suit academic and intellectual innovation and thought. The German educational system ultimately nurtures pupils to retain and employ these techniques as living competencies that, unlike the mere memorization and application of content, the German process builds a superseding and intuitive ability within its students to use the very methods and means of its instruction to apply to their approach to content. In essence, they learn how to learn. The strength of the program lies in that fact that content does not remain anchored in time or by grade level; rather, it becomes a part of the student's living memory because of the content's transition through the infrastructure's delivery. Content becomes connection; it becomes a part of the infrastructure process. The student can retain more knowledge because the mechanisms of reception are so thorough.

What is the reason why German education is esteemed in North and South America, Africa, Asia, Europe, and the Middle East? The medium of the message is grounded in the German language, but this is only one component of the promise of this educational standard. The transmission of cultural virtues might be framed through a Germanic prospective, but it is co-opted and reconciled by the host nation's students into their own cultural prospective. The German educational approach evolves into an international satellite because, while other cultural interpretations of it will utilize it to their ends, they will have at their cores an infrastructure, which is wholly transferable to any nation across the planet. A student educated by a German school in the Middle East will have gone through the same hybridization that occurs in Canada, but it is the core tenet of the methods and means that remains unchanged, regardless of national geography. That is precisely why the German model is an international education! Germany wishes the German Schools Abroad to be so called "Begegnunsschulen"—there is no real translation for this word—it is schools that emphasize and embrace cultural diversity and schools that nurture and promote connections. Connections are supposed to be made at these schools.

When parents begin to think about their child's education and their place in the 21st Century, the international century, they have begun to look beyond the traditional staged approach to education. Finding the right elementary school, enjoying and engaging that experience, then the correct secondary school, and ultimately the best suited post-secondary has changed for many families. Current educational international and domestic models are repositioning familial thinking in regards to this traditional approach. There is an increasing emphasis on what many would call the long-game or, perhaps, the end-game. In addition to the manifestation of the core tenets of a German international education, there also exists the intriguing dynamic of a conscious thought process which rests on achievement, career, and life goals. Unlike a staged approach, the German philosophy builds bridges into the future, recognizing the autonomy and dignity of the individual, but managing their perceived outcomes through the entire process. Psychologically, this is a significant positive because it sets a high standard of expectation, but also a mantra for success. They wouldn't speak to a kindergarten student or parent about their options for post-doctoral work, but visual, auditory, and other representations of what is expected, and more importantly, what is possible are part of the living language of instruction and the school's environment. The German International School of Toronto can shape this brilliant future for a child. They offer the best of the Canadian curriculum, fused with the methods and means required to make a child an international student in an international century. Begin with the word connection, and discover a portal to the future and the child's success.

Mom and Dad . . . I'm Bored

It often depends where this statement is announced and under which circumstances. Certainly, if it is coming from some course that a child is taking, then perhaps the lines of communication need to be opened between the teacher and the home. This is not necessarily what this article is about. Boredom is a natural state of the human mind, especially in children. It signifies a number of positive and negative thought patterns. Positively, it means that the mind has come to a fork in the road, where a major decision might be required, or the expanse of knowledge and experience has come to its logical and temporal conclusion. On the negative side, boredom identifies a lack of stimulation, inspiration, and the ability to self-engage and self-entertain. Whether it is a positive or negative situation, the ultimate result, for the student, would be to "snap out of it." Boredom has at its root cause the decision making process and the ability to make choices in concert with others, and more importantly, by one's self. The release of boredom is the exercise of freedom with responsibility.

Although it can never be found anywhere in the Ontario Curriculum as a defined competency, a comprehensive elementary education must include the explicit and implicit means by which children are taught to decide independently. The wonderful aspect at this level of instruction is that one's decisions in the classroom really do not have long lasting effects; they might be incorrect answers or missteps, but this is how students learn to think for themselves. Our Language Arts program at Northmount School operates under one such paradigm: gradual release. It is the transfer of literacy from direct instruction with students not possessing the text, to text based inquiry, to group work, and eventual independent reading, but with the intellectual tools to discern meaning and examine a book deeper than its base plot lines. The same concept is easily transferable to some of the social abilities, conventions, and graces being taught in the home and at school.

Decision making also rests heavily upon the child's ability to cope with adversity and crisis. While those two terms might have an extreme tone; boredom and its close cousin frustration, are aspects of the human condition children need to learn to deal with more independently. What an adult might regard as a crisis can be far different than that which a child might perceive. The grand mission of social education is to bring reasonable parity between the perceptions and choices of children and that of adults. Children who lack the ability to think for themselves and know they can always get an immediate rectification to their "crisis" are going to incur difficulty as adolescents and certainly as adults. **Decisiveness is a declining quality of the early 21st century, and as it casts its shadow of doubt, incompetence, and irresponsibility many persons are damaged in its wake.** The origin of the scourge of indecisiveness is the ability to stand behind one's convictions and choices and to wield thought as a means of freedom.

Decisive individuals have shaped the course of human history. When done with the aid of a moral compass, the results are spectacular, as in the case of Dr. Martin Luther King Jr. However, dithering and indecisive leadership has been the ruin of many states and organizations, take for example the sovereignty debt crisis of Europe. Those macro decisions all had their genesis in the education and experience of the people who made them. If we wish our children to be informed, moral, and decisive persons; we must allow them to fail, make their own decisions, teach them how to assess risk, and not shy away from situations that are not always guaranteed. The easiness of the escape hatch or clause has perpetuated a disturbing social ethos that suggests anything can be gotten out of or easily quit. Education and parenting that fosters independence as an end goal will undoubtedly reverse the trend. Being bored is not a prerequisite to quitting, but an invitation to cope and attain success.

The Intervention of Masculinity

Recently, while at a friend's home, I had the opportunity to observe a rather fascinating dynamic unfold. Their son, in grade nine, was now on to his third high school in six months, and there were some signs of anxiety surrounding this last option. I inquired as to the nature of the problems their son was facing with these schools. The first one, a vocational school, had an excellent 'sales pitch' but in reality was plagued by severe behaviour issues and inability to meet the needs of this young man. After that choice, the second school proved to be far too advanced with an emphasis solely on the academic stream. The previous two selections also reported some friendship and social adjustment complaints from the boy. The third school they had found seemed to be a perfect fit with the right attention and mixture of applied and vocational courses. However, their son was now beginning to bristle. His mother had led the effort in these choices, meeting with principals and discovering the curriculum of each of these three very different schools. She had produced a monumental effort for her son. What played out in the room was fascinating. The female members of the family all surrounded this young man, and offered him hugs and support, while the male members appeared to wait in the wings for the ideal moment. His father and his uncle, waited for the women to leave and then, each in turn, as an aside spoke to him. Their tone was different, still infused with empathy, but altered by a sense of practical advice that frankly, went beyond suggestion, but stopped short of command. Their words with him dealt with getting tough, having to deal with situations, facing up instead of running away, and basically facing the lions and how to tap into internal fortitude. This was the intervention of masculinity.

Before you perceive this article as turning into a female vs. male diatribe, let me assure it is not. Make no mistake; women wield masculinity in their own right. I can attest that fact to my two German grandmothers. My mother was another. Strong women have, and will continue to be at the core of the family. Many, due to circumstances beyond their control, have had to play both genders' strengths and have been admirable at doing so. However, young males do seek out other males for many different reasons. There is an undeniable authenticity to an interaction between males of the same, and different ages. Educational psychologists have posited that young males look for other classmates to define, reinforce, and establish an early sense of masculinity and social identity. Dr. Leonard Sax suggested that male children and adolescents are lacking, what he called the "loss of the traditional gods." Dr. Sax referred to the simple witnessing of older males performing labour in the home and in the workplace. Masculine inner fortitude was always nicely mirrored by sons watching peers, older male siblings, uncles, cousins, and fathers labouring, failing and ultimately succeeding.

There still remains this masculinity that requires some definition. Unfortunately, true masculinity has been lampooned, discounted, and defined as inferior and not equal to a wiser sense of femininity, while it has its place as an equal, is also diminished when its alter ego has been damaged. How then do we define masculinity? A few universal themes come to mind: perseverance, calculated risk, boldness, swift conflict resolution, empathy, notions of male competition (improving ones competitors then playing), rank, chivalry, leadership, and exercising the beauty of strength. There are mental assertions of masculinity as well, they include: the assertion of dignity, giving one's word, treating women with respect and equality, making sacrifices, and steadfastness in the face of extreme conditions (bravery).

We are progressing toward a comprehension of the two genders that has traversed the spectrum from mere understanding and documentation, to legitimate social behaviours in the West. Our greatest folly would be to define equality as a symbiosis of the genders into one social mode of behaviour and conduct. Female and male, femininity and masculinity can be practiced by opposite genders, yet, there still remains the undeniable truth that the authenticity of example, is, and will forever, continue to be relevant and worthy of the phrase "Viva la difference." Young men search for the authentic and the genuine in their self-definition of masculinity. Male perpetuation and transmission of the masculine values and their influence on self-perception is a large part of the equation, one we know is unique and forged at Northmount.

Where am I?

Try this experiment. Take a piece of paper and ask your son to draw a small picture of your house. Then have him draw your street, neighbourhood, community, and perhaps even city. The investigation of spatial intelligence through the use of "mental maps", maps produced by a subject from pure recognition and memory is quite telling in regards to a child's understanding of his or her environment. Most parents who attempt this project with their children are surprised both negatively and positively by the results. However, what becomes abundantly clear is that many children have a very limited knowledge of their immediate surroundings and their community. We can easily discount this finding by stating that our children are not old enough to go roaming around the neighbourhood and discovering their community. There are some incontrovertible truths, which stand in opposition to our own disagreement: our children are growing and often through curiosity they can lose their sense of direction and sheer panic can quickly become a reality.

Try another challenge. Ask your children if they know the major intersection (you may have to put this in simpler terms) and what their nearest store might be. While I can recall the heady days of street hockey and being with my friends in the park; it is a melancholy truth that this generation of children has had safe space defined for them by factors my generation did not have to contend with, or if we did, not in the same severity. The loss for this generation of children, aside from the fun and frivolity of the street, is the sense of awareness of community and neighbourhood. While I do believe this can be recaptured in adolescence and certainly in adulthood, it does craft a sense of isolation that could affect the maintenance of diverse and engaging communities within the city. The essence of this article has been what was traditionally held as the side-effects of street proofing, but offers a unique pathway toward that behaviour/habit forming exercise in less of a threatening presuppose. The specters of the distrusted stranger offering candy and the fear of certain places often don't make for good introductions to this type of education best offered in the home, but certainly complimented in the school.

A lost or missing child is every parent's nightmare. A prepared child who has some sense of their immediate space and the correct behaviours to deal with crisis situations is a major asset. Statistically, we can take great comfort in the fact that our children are not likely to be abducted, but we can also delve deeper into these figures and identify a discernable inverse relationship regarding abduction and street proofing. Knowledge is power, even for children. Your introduction to their street, neighbourhood, and community will temper their behavioural responses to such simple things as identifying the roads leading into their respective areas and recognizing community landmarks. Other benefits will arise in the form of confidence, self-esteem, family exercise time when walking through the neighbourhood, and a further sense of belonging. While we can lament the passing of street hockey, the many parent eyes on children, and the loss or severe contraction of programs like Neighbourhood Watch; we can, like the fire drills in school, ingrain a response for being lost that is noticeably less anxious and more systematic in the coping mechanisms of the child. There is much we can teach your child, but negotiating the spaces between and the knowledge to deal with crisis is the stewardship of the parent. Frame the world through your eyes and responses, and the picture will be a masterpiece.

When in Roam

I am not sure exactly when it occurred, but probably around the time when some Generation X (1965-1985) and early Generation Y (1978-1990) became parents. There seemed to be a **contraction in childhood geo-graphical space**, freedom, responsibility, and the ability to make independent decisions without the full input of parents. The term helicopter parent comes to mind. It was originally coined by Foster W. Cline, M.D. and Jim Fay in their 1990 book *Parenting with Love and Logic: Teaching Children Responsibility.* It is essentially the intervention of parents in every aspect of the child's life removing any obstacles that might challenge or through parental perception, harm their offspring. Helicoptered children are unable to independently reason for them-selves in times of crisis, under normal circumstances, and when called upon by their peers and teachers to do so. The emotional and psychological ramifications of such practices have given rise to mass insecurity/anxiety, a generation of children who seek non-competitive environments and no-harm, no-foul pursuits like the emptiness of video games. The—Life Coach has also emerged as the de facto parent or nanny that parachutes into the adolescent and early adulthood lives of helicopter children. What has also become quite apparent is the loss of freedom on the physical plain of the world. Take a drive through some of your local neighbourhoods. Are teens playing street hockey? Exactly who is in the parks? Where are today's youth?

A 2009 article in Britain's *Daily Mail* on the distance different generations could travel at age 8 noted the following:

*"When George Thomas was eight he walked everywhere. It was 1926 and his parents were unable to afford the fare for a tram, let alone the cost of a bike and he regularly walked six miles (9.656064 kilometers) to his favorite fishing haunt without adult supervision. His son-in-law, Jack Hattersley, 63, was also given freedom to roam. He was aged eight in 1950, and was allowed to walk for about one mile (1.609344 kilometers) on his own to the local woods. Again, he walked to school and never travelled by car. In 1979, his daughter could travel half a mile to the local pool. Fast forward to 2007 and Mr. Thomas's eight-year-old great-grandson Edward enjoys none of that freedom. He is driven the few minutes to school, is taken by car to a safe place to ride his bike and can roam no more than 300 yards (274.32 meters) from home."*1

While this data was taken from Sheffield, England let us take those same figures and apply it to a neighbourhood in North York that begins as its centre, Northmount School. There will of course be sociological differences and urban realities in the translation, however, the results are still quite telling. 1969 over fifty percent of school children got there by walking or bicycling. Today only thirteen percent of kids get to school on their own power.2 Several neighbourhood schools, which I had the opportunity to study in East End Toronto, had increased motor traffic over the past twenty years. What were once schools that had droves of children walking through the local streets now had a cue of cars lined up to drop-off and pick-up children. Although an American study, the graph below corroborates much of the anecdotal information from local Toronto schools. In 1969, over fifty percent of school children got there by walking or bicycling. Today only thirteen percent of kids get to school on their own power.

Arguably, the dynamic for an independent school and its families are operating under alternate circumstances then perhaps that of the local neighbourhood school. However, upon closer examination, the two entities are now behaving remarkably similar. The catchment zone for the independent school is initially larger than that of the community oriented public school, but as they establish themselves in their local neighbourhoods, the independent schools appear to draw more from their immediate geographic zones of influence then perhaps they did at their inception. Society and spatial connections (interpretations, perceptions, and executions of space) have trans-formed dramatically over the past twenty years. **Space and time have both contracted and expanded.**

Some children in the early 21st Century have reverted to a type of 19th Century retro definition of children as being miniature adults. The key differentiator being that their historical counterparts only negotiated physical space. 21st Century children do the same with the following variables: an over-programmed and fast-paced urban environment and a limitless new definition of space-cyberspace. If one were to repeat the exercise of Figure 2.0 with these two components, the physical plain of occupation might further contract, but the outlier geographic data for specific points of engagement (lessons, leagues, clubs, athletics, and family) would surge beyond that of the 19th and early 20th Century child's zones of familiarity. The fourth dimension of cyberspace is the creation of limitless places, not grounded to the physical plain, yet one critical factor in its demise.

The challenge for this century's parents will be to fashion a framing of experience that is inclusive of this fourth dimension, yet not wholly dictated by it. Children must have authentic responsibility anchored in the reality of the physical plain and governed by real relationships. Scenarios that might present obstacles, heart ache, and pain; yet, provide the stuff that the human condition has raged against and triumphed over through success is essential in the creation of a well-balanced and independent adult. How fascinating is it that in 110 years, the term roaming has de-evolved from an autonomous movement synonymous with exploration to the safety of the virtual tether (an umbilical cord of sorts) offered by the cell phone?

The T.T.C. Club and Other Pursuits

What you put into school is what you get out of it. This was a central theme to my Grade 9 year at Francis Libermann Catholic High in 1984-85. A then, very svelte "niner" listened intently as his science teacher, Mr. Beck coined the term, "The T.T.C. Club." He began to speak of it in this manner. To quote, *"Libermann and all other schools in Toronto all share in one of the biggest clubs in whole city; our chapter is one of the leading branches. Most of us meet at the bus stop around 3:15 p.m. and instead of building new members, as the afternoon progresses, the club gets smaller and smaller until no one is left. Don't join, but become involved in school life out-side of classes, high school will be a brilliant experience if you do*!" Many of us took his message to heart, trying out for sports teams, acquainting ourselves with a host of various clubs, playing in the concert band, and definite-ly going to dances. Yours truly joined the cross-country team, and while it was well beyond my capabilities as an athlete, and I use the term sparingly; it did open up some new realities for me. These notable observations included: never asking your former CFL player, gym teacher if you could sit out today's class as you had a meet at night, this resulted in jogging around the Brimley Woods for 75 minutes, nor, at the last meet of the year, running while simultaneously eating a bag of chips; a reputation, which still haunts me today as I was reminded by Libermann's principal (former cross-country coach), two years ago, on a Knight's of Columbus visit to my old alma mater. Truth be told, it was a great experience and it expanded by friendship base three fold, while instructing me in the finer points of perseverance! Especially, when, then principal, Mr. J.P. Patenuade made a point of recognizing the cross-country team on the morning announcements, after taking the time to speak to me in the hall, after a heavily mud laden practice.

I made a point in asking as many of our Grade 7 and 8 students if they were going to the St. Clement's dance. The dance experience is so important to general life moments and memories, and it is also somewhat of a "rite of passage" for adolescents to go through. While it can have its great successes and some set-backs, to deny young people this experience is to take something away from them that assists with the building blocks of socialization and ultimately sound lessons in a controlled environment, with mixed gender company and court-ship. Mr. Beck's words would ring in our minds when my friends and I bought tickets for high school dances, which were always sold out. One of our English teachers, who had a particularly rapier wit, often instructed us guys on how to ask a young lady for a dance. Once, a friend of mine posed the question, "What if they say no?" His response was, "Just laugh, they won't know what it means and you'll feel better." Sort of sums up the whole seriousness and angst of dances. We would all make a point of attending these parties and putting "our cool" on the line. Another good friend of mine, who is now a police officer had a strategy of dancing near girls and sing-ing the particular song being played at the moment, the only problem was that he was easily distracted. So when the slow song entitled, "I miss you like crazy" came on, he sang out loud, "I guess you like gravy." Being involved in school does have its ups and downs, but it's those memories that make it all count!

Social justice was a big theme at Libermann. The aforementioned crooner had been interested in a fellow class-mate during Grade 12, who encouraged him to come and help her with the homeless at The Good Sheppard Refuge on Queen St. East. He knew that the boys and I would be reluctant to go for a myriad of reasons, but he did not want to go alone. For some reason he was able to convince me to come along. For six months, while he courted this girl, I bussed tables, scarped plates, cut pies, and talked to a lot of people from all walks of life (a cause that still remains with me). At the final awards assembly that year, predictably, my friend's girlfriend won an award and stated to all of us in a rather condescending tone, which she had become infamous for, "Maybe if you guys worked a bit harder, you might win something too!" Then it happened. A long-time favorite History teacher of ours came to the podium and announced that my friend and I had won the Christian Service Award! As he stated, "I can't believe this, but it's true." My pal Damian shouted out his loudest "WHOAAAAAAAAA" ever. It was a sweet victory, and truly another equally sweet memory of becoming involved in school life.

The Last Post

Nearly a year has passed since our last Remembrance Day ceremony. Soon the commemorative display will be mounted near the mural and parents and honoured guests will arrive to share in our evocation of memory at our service in the agora, save one. Last summer, my Father-in-Law, Earle Wilson Wong, passed away suddenly. Mr. Wong served in the Royal Air Force, in Cypress, through its turbulent era, during the late 1950's and early 1960's. Following this experience, he never attended any Remembrance Day events, choosing instead to keep the day in quiet contemplation at home. When invited to come to Northmount, he had some reservations.

Mr. Wong had long lamented the rapid diminishing standards and values in Canadian schools as they related to conduct, respect, and Christian values. He also spent much of the 1970's to the late 1990's, as an organizer of youth soccer in North York, hoping, in his own way, to make a difference in lives of Canadian youth and foster a sense of moral fortitude and manners. Mr. Wong encouraged fair play and honour amongst all of his charges. He worried that the ceremony would be filled with cacophonic outbursts of student laughter and talking, and that as a guest, he might be regarded only as an object of curiosity or even worse, amusement. From the moment he walked through the front door, he was greeted by two senior students who wished him a good morning, offered their personal thanks for his service, and took him to his seat with smiles on their faces. Mr. Wong want-ed, and had made a motion to sit with the general audience, but when invited to the front by Major General Guy Thibault, he just couldn't refuse. He also saw how dignified the agora had been designed for this special day.

The moment where his faith had to have been restored in today's youth, was when each and every student re-moved their poppy, placed it on the cross, and went to shake his hand, thanking him for his service in the R.A.F. I could see that emotion was beginning to take hold him as a smile and gleeful look in his eyes met every North-mount boy, family, and faculty member. Following the formalities, Mr. Wong was thrilled by the kindly treat-ment he received from all of the students: the way in which they outstretched their hands, said hello, and to his utter surprise, asked for his autograph. Above all, the boys took the time to hear his stories and ask meaningful questions. I thought that once the service had concluded, he would be on his way, but he made a point of staying for the student council induction portion of the morning. As he put on his characteristic hat, he leaned over to me and commented on his astonishment that such young boys could carry off such a venerable ceremony and how well they stood, with a quiet confidence reflecting the genuine appreciation they had for the veterans and their sacrifices.

Funny enough, Mr. Wong never spoke of that brief time at our school again. As he had never gone to these ceremonies before, I believed it closed a chapter in his life and gave him a glimpse, at a future, of a country he loved very much. His gift of service for the ultimate goal of freedom would finally be bequeathed to worthy recipients. His only communication about the event was in the form of a short email, in keeping with his style that read, "Thank you, it was great." This was his last email to me, his last post.

A Son-in-Law, with Eternal and Unshakeable Respect

Loneliness:
The Specter of Urban Life

Frederick Olmstead's design of the 19ᵗʰ Century's Central Park in New York during the Industrial Age was meant to act as a place to breathe and relax amidst the pollution of an emerging manufacturing colossus. The park was a respite for the weary factory worker who could not afford the more pleasant surroundings of upstate New York. No doubt, the park was also a place to socialize and be with family. Sociologists of the time suggested that the sudden rush to dense urban living was contrary to social evolution and the maturation of the human condition; while the body would accept the changes, the human soul would be hard pressed to acclimatize. It would seem this would be the genesis of the ultimate paradox; more togetherness seemed to create a cloak of invisibility around persons whom we, to coin an early 21ˢᵗ Century saying, were not in our calling circle. The paradox employs anonymity, the cold rapidity of technology, and the theft of time's true meaning.

Rural life as it's romanticized by city folk tends to be about community values and a sense of belonging; while those who hail from the experience will lament the negativity of one's neighbors being privy to every bit of minutia from grocery brands purchased to family intrigue. Somewhere in between is what historian Michael Kammen suggested as, "The tradition of a collective memory in history that serves innovative causes like spirituality." This collective memory is not something which was necessarily grounded in the past, but can be an active catalyst in modern life if its membership is restricted.

Has modernity changed us all into post-modern historians quietly putting together our own fully annotated account of The Complete Nation of . . . . (fill in your name)? Selfishness coupled with instant gratification and celebrity has deceived us all. We wield the anonymous climate of the city for both good and evil ends, while accountability and originality are discarded as useless past times. It is this anonymous nature of the city that excuses direct involvement in the plight of the poor, oppressed, and the victimized; "someone will take care of them." More sinister to the undistinguished character of the city is its nameless reference for truth, "they said those people were like that." Anonymity excludes and marginalizes people who turn inward and have loneliness embrace them.

Journalist Freeman Tilden wrote, "We have always known in our inner most recesses that our dependence on beauty has given us the courage to face the problems of life. We have let ourselves forget that." Tilden's beauty is that of the human being and our spark of divinity, which will be glimpsed on occasion while its potential is envisioned by philosophers, dreamers, and poets. The cold rapid delivery of technology has taken from us the delight and the horror of the human experience and replaced it with a commonplace existence of mediocre emotional response. Imagine a newscast where the presenter was not so disengaged from the material being covered and reacted with emotion to each segment. Could this be why we are so jolted when an interview shows men and women weeping openly on the six o'clock news? The magnitude of death and our sympathies toward it have been made numb by the sheer volume of violent acts and the anonymity of persons outside our daily routines. Technology's use of disposable language for media sound bites is equally culpable. "At risk youth", living in "at risk neighborhoods", possibly becoming "at risk offenders" make it a "risky" proposition for others willing to ask the question, "How can I help?" Paranoia is the other side of the coin of loneliness.

There is no difference in the amount of time that you may have compared to that of your neighbor, its twenty-four hours for everyone. The critical aspect remains, how will you spend it? Most of it is already owing to career and supporting one's family; both laudable activities, but what about the pursuit of happiness? Has it been confused with indifferent acquisition and consumer competition? Having taught children from all economic strata, all they want is their parents' time. I use to have a teacher would repeatedly recall the phrase "Time is of the essence". This came across, to a then elementary school student as "hurry up!" In fact, it resonates differently in adulthood as time is precious and one should not treat is as fleeting. There is a particular depression of spirit when it is realized that every moment of the day is already spoken for before its commencement or the opposite, that there is plenty of time with no meaningful fulfillment existing in its endless chasm.

Christ calls us to see him in all of humanity. The artificial constructs of time, perception, language, value, and landscape are transcended by the consciousness of the spirit. What happens in God's time does often not match what we want in our time. We too can also peer through this existential window with Christ, if we open our minds to a sort of spiritual deconstruction of the urban landscape which has been pulled over our eyes like a veil. The Christian should look beyond perception, question what has been deemed acceptable and challenge these notions of social construction as Christ did. They will discover that loneliness and its accompanying ghosts are mere transparent specters clouding the judgment of the urban dweller.

Moral Education:
Teaching Religion to a
Faith-Diverse Student Body

Prospective parents, representing a myriad of faith backgrounds, often ask how the Northmount School religion program works and which model is used. Evangelization through doctrinal insistence of faith, practice and dogmatic mantras is most definitely not the way to achieve effective delivery of religious education, whether to a homogeneous group of believers or a collective group of eager yet diverse minds. In fact, the delivery of a moral education, grounded in the truths and practices of the Roman Catholic Church, does not begin in the classroom at all. Its genesis lies in the atmosphere of the school and its own inalienable tenets of service and virtue through instruction and, more critically, through genuine example.

THE WAY

Persons of faith, regardless of denomination, sect or variance of belief, have nothing to fear from other persons of faith. However, the moral principles and religious goals of the institution with regard to its mandate must be clearly and unequivocally stated in print, electronic media and verbal transmission. Northmount School's statement of faith education is: "Northmount wishes each student to be the best adherent of the faith tradition of the family." Our single-faith school regards parents as the primary educators of their children; our partnership is thus echoed in academia, social graces, and the teaching, maintenance and fostering of religious conviction. A former headmaster was once asked, "Why would non-Catholic parents choose to send their sons to Northmount?" His answer: "For the roots, or the fruits."

Many would regard a faith-diverse student body and the nature of Catholic religious tradition as an insurmountable paradox. It is not. Vatican II stated that,

The Catholic Church rejects nothing that is true and holy in these religions [monotheist and Eastern]. She regards with sincere reverence those ways of conduct and of life, those precepts and teachings which, though differing in many aspects from the ones she holds and sets forth, nonetheless often reflect a ray of that Truth which enlightens all men. Indeed, she proclaims, and ever must proclaim Christ "the way, the truth, and the life" (John 14:6), in whom men may find the fullness of religious life, in whom God has reconciled all things to Himself. The Church therefore, exhorts her sons, that through dialogue and collaboration with the followers of other religions, carried out with prudence and love and in witness to the Christian faith and life, they ***recognize, preserve and promote the good things, spiritual and moral***

The fear of conversion or religious superiority is again raised as a countervailing reason for avoiding schools based on one religion's teachings. Vatican II sought to repair and reconcile the relationships between the Roman Catholic Church and other Christian and non-Christian faiths. The differences are there, upheld and accepted; our mission is to enter a legitimate conversation about the rule of God and how this can be interpreted and universally binding to everyone.

THE TRUTH

Critics will suggest that this total acceptance of all faith traditions is only possible under the two following assumptions: that one Faith tradition is de facto superior and trumps all others leaving the individual to reconcile dogmatic differences and practices, and that a wholly artificial relativism exists that posits all faiths as equal with no room for a critical examination, which may yield positive or negative commentary (disingenuous political correctness).

The Northmount paradigm is different. It puts forth the foundation of a Catholic religious education, not steeped in evangelization but focused in the more cerebral delivery of history, theology and the consequences of a moral life. Grounded in the beliefs and traditions of the Roman Catholic Church, it is easily transferable and inclusive of other faith traditions. Central to the atmosphere in a religion class are catechetical instruction for Roman Catholics, and the education of all students on Catholic culture and the universal values of love, kindness, compassion and respect for the dignity of life.

Relativism would compromise Northmount's core values and, more severely, dilute its own operational truths. Our living example is to hold true to Roman Catholic principles and standards. This causes a true hermeneutic circle of influence and meaning because student adherents of other faith traditions learn the same resolve.

Genuine discussions of faith can only occur when all parties hold true to their own principles and beliefs. Thus, the discussion evolves from a persuasive-/conversion-style dialogue to one that seeks genuine truth through approaches to moral living. What further develops is the advent of principled and balanced discussion anchored in the ethos of appreciation and encouragement of all faith traditions guided by their respective moral compasses. Simply put, a virtuous character educated by morality, guided by faith and practice, and resting on an unshakeable and non-negotiable foundation can only emerge.

THE LIFE

Beyond the theological is the application of faith through practice. A central tenet of a school that espouses a particular faith yet welcomes all others is universal physical manifestations, of which all members of the community become emotional stakeholders.

Northmount School offers a program of social assistance within the context of the community, province, nation and globe. Helping the needy and visiting the aged and infirm are two such initiatives that, while certainly grounded in Catholic tradition, are explicitly stated in the practical behaviours of most of the world's faiths. Activities include giving food hampers, playing bingo with senior citizens, raising money and supplies for developing world literacy programs, and helping orphanages and institutions that support life and human dignity. For the student, it is replacing attitude with gratitude.

Lost in early 21st-century leadership are compassion and empathy that include a spiritual dimension. Faith-based schools incorporate the human qualities in their definition of leadership and governance. Arguably, the question of religious competition is quelled by a culture not simply of toleration (tacit secular approval) but of true acceptance of everyone as a child of God, having human dignity of incalculable value. The potential of a child is then measured not by the limited boundaries of academia but by the true unbounded nature of the spiritual realm.

Within a religious environment, notions of authority and consequence become factors in the formation of a moral character. The Catholic tradition is crystal clear about moral codes and discipline; Catholic education is known for its brand of corrective character nurturing.

True morality, espoused by Northmount School to parents, is that their sons "must know the good, and do the good when no one is around." Accountability in a morally sound atmosphere is acceptance not just of the temporal authority (parent, teacher and administration), which can forgive and punish at the same time, but also of a spiritual consciousness that rewards, punishes and forgives in its own time (the temporal authorities are the only ones that can be negotiated with). Essentially, it is a mindset that embodies a "second thought of consequence" for the student. This pays huge dividends in the establishment of a culture of respect. All faiths recognize that a morally educated student should inherit a fear of authority—not an unhealthy cowering, but the notion that doing wrong would result in the disappointment of temporal and spiritual authorities. In essence, they develop an empathetic, self-regulating conscience.

At a pedagogical level, intervention comes by way of a Northmount adviser for each student and his family. As a coach of sorts, advisers work on a virtue, prescribed monthly for the entire school. Goals are set, verified, discussed and enacted by the student. There is a living conversation between the home and the school. Aside from academic goals being mirrored by both, once virtue and habit are in tandem, the degree of parallel objectives produces a student and an atmosphere that foster the drive to become extraordinary in every domain of life. Educators often comment that if one-on-one instruction can be delivered, the scope of understanding and internalizing of knowledge and wisdom will be much more prolific. Faith and virtue are no exception. Every individual has a very personal relationship with his or her own faith tradition. The promise of the Advisory Program is fulfilled in the emotional well-being of the student. Our boys feel that they belong, they contribute and they all have a voice that is heard—a testament to acceptance of their diversity.

A father recently told me that he wants two things for his son: to be successful in school and life, and to be someone he can be proud of as an adult. The twin tenets of leadership and service resonate with all of the faiths at Northmount School. Families wish their sons to become men of conviction, courage and resolute steadfastness to the truth. If an institution cannot rest upon its own faith foundations, it cannot hope to transfer this commitment to principles to its constituency. *Libertas in Veritate*—freedom in truth—is the school's motto. Security in one's standards and beliefs allows for the genuine dissemination and learning of a guiding morality and virtue that, while securely anchored in one faith tradition, shine a shepherding light down our diverse paths toward salvation and enlightenment.

Who's Afraid of Halloween?

When I was growing up I can remember being so excited about going out and trick-or-treating. Images of costumes that didn't quite fit, reduced vision and streets full of parents accompanying their children to neighbours' houses resound in my memory.

I can also recall several friends who were Catholic, Christian and some other faiths shunning this activity, citing its connection with evil. Being under the age of 10, I didn't quite grasp that at the time, I always thought they were talking about the danger of cavities, finding a razor blade in an apple or being assaulted for candy. Now I know better.

However, the question of why this link exists to something sinister such as the occult or Satan has intrigued me for a while. Is Halloween the festival of dark forces and the glorification of Satan that many fundamentalists would swear it to be?

A cursory look at some of the ghoulish costumes would generate a yes. However, an examination of the celebration's history denotes a more measured response. According to many historical sources, including the Catholic Dictionary, Halloween traces its origins back to the ancient Celts. The advent of winter and the Celtic new year was Nov. 1. The festival of Samhain, Lord of the Dead, was celebrated on New Year's Eve. "Celts believed the souls of the dead—including ghosts, goblins and witches—returned to mingle with the living. In order to scare away the evil spirits, people would wear masks and light bonfires."

When the Romans conquered the Celts, they added making centrepieces out of apples and nuts for Pomona, the Roman goddess of the orchards. The Romans also bobbed for apples and drank cider. In 835, Pope Gregory IV moved the celebration for all the martyrs (later all saints) from May 13 to Nov. 1. The night before became known as All Hallow's Eve or "holy evening."

Eventually the name was shortened to the current Halloween. On Nov. 2, the church celebrated All Souls Day. "The purpose of those feasts was to remember those who had died, whether they were officially recognized by the church as saints or not. It was a celebration of the 'communion of saints,' which reminds us that the church was not bound by space or time."

Many Catholics I have spoken with have recalled moments in their parish and student lives when they had been encouraged to dress as saints or martyrs; the wonderful aspect of this was that all of the macabre costuming was still there and then some. Our saints and martyrs died in some truly horrific circumstances, holding steadfast to their faith in the face of unimaginable malice and certain death. One gentleman recalled seeing a boy dressed up as St. Thomas More with his head in hands. Yikes!

Christians should know that one of the pillars of our faith is the triumph over evil and death; it began with Lucifer defying God and being cast from Heaven, Christ rejecting His temptation in the desert and then as the originally worded creed denoted, "Died for our sins, descended to hell (modern: the Dead) and then rose again." Being a Christian means recognizing that death is everywhere, but we should not fear it as we have been delivered from it by Christ and our faith in Him. Some would suggest that Halloween is in fact a celebration of this spiritual triumph; a mocking of the occult and a recognition that it is in no way equal to the power of God.

According to the American Catholic, "A later custom developed where people would go door-to-door on Nov. 2, requesting small cakes in exchange for the promise of saying prayers for some of the dead relatives of each house. This arose out of the religious belief that the dead were in a state of limbo before they went to heaven or hell and that the prayers of the living could influence the outcome. This may have been the precursor to Trick-or Treat." As a priest once said to my students, "Have fun with Halloween, don't take it seriously, and most importantly remember the solemnity of All Souls and All Saints Day."

If we want to take the true "evil" out of Halloween, turn on our lights, accompany our children, be vigilant in our supervision and build upon our community by meeting a few neighbours. The seriousness of life and benediction of the honoured dead will, too, have its rightful place in November.

Keeping Time at Christmas

A good friend of mine once told me that most people are of the "can't wait variety." They lament the present moment that they are in, and long for some future day or event. Often when the event arrives, it may or may not de-liver upon its expectations, but most certainly fades into memory. Until the next "can't wait event" manifests it-self, the individual is left with a sense of emptiness, longing, or even despair. It is very easy to fall into those minefields of the human condition, if we have tethered ourselves too closely to the temporal and artificial realm of the physical plain. If you feel that you want to get off the merry-go-round, it might be time to take a moment and engage your emotional and spiritual side. For some, this might include a religious retreat, and for others, a time-out, where they may wish to take stock of all of the wonderful gifts and blessings they have in their own lives. The serious cases begin to put on the brakes, when they can actually see themselves doing the wrong thing or pursuing a manic course of action, which is only broken by the most interrogative of questions, "Just what am I doing?" For me those questions and putting on the brakes seem to occur most often in Church. This past Sun-day, the Gospel encouraged us to be open and accepting of Jesus' coming and above all, to trust in the Lord and know that our Faith will fulfill all of the promises of salvation. What changed my outlook was not necessarily the Gospel, but a banner near the sacristy that simply stated, "Lord, Change My Heart."

I am a worrier. I know that there are many like me out there. I worry even when there is nothing to worry about. I worry about the fact that there is nothing to worry about, and why I am not worried about that; surely there must be something? My wife, who is a Baptist, will now and then ask me to accompany her to her Church. Being of an ecumenical mind, interested in other denominations of Christianity, and always eager to please my mother-in-law, I accompany her, of course wearing my Knights of Columbus tie. Pastor Bruce, has admittedly, delivered some of the finest sermons regarding Christian living that I have ever heard. While I do quibble with his take on theological issues, as they are filtered through my Catholicity; his notion of time, faith, and worry were beautifully expressed in a recent oration. "We should never worry too much, because as people of faith, our final destination, on our journey, will always end with Jesus; and he keeps time." There is a great deal of security and peace in such a realization. Father Dexter, a visiting priest to St. Bartholomew's Church, from Trinidad, used to say that, "Our worries are our own King Harrods; they temporarily block us from what we need most, but overcoming these obstacles, whether they be physical, mental, emotional, or spiritual, are part and parcel of living a Christ-centered life." These reflections help us to unwind.

There are of course other times when perhaps God sends us more of a direct and personal message. Recently, some members of my family attended an antique auction; a pastime the family has enjoyed for many years. As I was speaking to my aunt, she asked if I had seen the brass clock with real-time movement on our way into the auction house. I had. Inquisitively, she questioned me if it had reminded me of anything. Of course it had. I immediately responded with, "Yes, it was just like Granny's clock from Germany that she would have me wind in her bedroom when she was alive." I also told her I never knew what happened to it after she died. My aunt simply smiled. The next day at our rotating family Advent Sunday's, my uncle carried in a solid brass, real-time movement, and glass domed clock. He motioned to me, "Since we're moving, we thought that you would treasure this from Granny most of all." Gently, I took it from them and told them it meant the world to me. Once I was home, I dusted it off and remembered my Granny's words of advice, *"Nict so eng."* "Not so tight." I had al-ways wanted the clock to move and time to race forward. Perhaps now, the message rang truer, "Not so tight, not so fast, enjoy the moment and have faith."

Hope in a Box

A mother and son arrived on a blustery winter day. The competition had already begun and she hurried to get him ready. As I glanced at the student, he was in full athletic gear, with the exception of his shoes. He hurried to take off his coat and hat. The young man opened his knapsack and inside was a box in which he carefully stored his new running shoes. He unpacked them, gingerly removing the tissue and placing them on the gym floor. His eyes glanced over at some of his friends, and he nodded as if to acknowledge the fact that he was ready to compete and had brought his best. I recalled that this was the same type of thing my friends and I did some twenty years ago. The experience of first generation immigrants had echoed through time. It was emotional to witness this again. The Scarborough District 87 Free Throw was so special, that a new pair of shoes had to be purchased. I also knew from personal experience that other items had to have been deferred in order to make this possible.

We often forget some of the pivotal moments of our youth, yet life has a fascinating way of reminding us of these times through similar events. The impact of the Knights of Columbus Free Throw Tournament was such a moment. As adults we have complicated and multi-dimensional lives. Aspects of what we place as important and relevant are spread throughout multiple places of interaction with others. Children place far greater emphasis on events as their world is much smaller. Yet, there are moments of convergence when both worlds regard something as being worthy of attention. This is precisely why the Knights of Columbus Free Throw Tournament is so significant because the community has deemed this an important event and we too, as the organizers treated it accordingly.

Arriving a half an hour before the commencement of the Free Throw, a father and son came through the front door of Northmount School. The father had with him a camera and was carrying his teenage son's bag. They asked me if they could go into the gym and begin to practice. I guided them to the gymnasium, where moments later I would see the dad actually rebounding the ball to his son while giving him tips on how to shoot and obtain good posture. With each word of encouragement, the father also mentioned some form of physical position that his son might use to help his game. Anxiously the father waited and watched, prompted his son when needed and carefully scouted the other boys who would be playing against his son. As the tournament wore on, he graciously asked as to what time the program would end. He predicated the question by adding that he had taken off some time from his day job, but did not want to be late for his evening employment. He looked tired, shoulders heavy with wincing eyes. He said he would wait and did, taking photos and speaking with his son.

It was heart-warming to witness the number of parents attending. They brought cameras, other relatives, and friends. It was an occasion that involved the family. Teachers from the Toronto Catholic District School Board also attended and spoke to their representative students with similar parental care and concern. As an independent Catholic School in North York, it was Northmount School's pleasure to provide a facility for this tournament. The audience was pensive and responsive to each and every shot on the basket. They reacted to tie-breaking situations and of moments of angst and joy from the competitors. I could see parents wringing their hands and holding on to their spouses and children as one of their own was commencing to take another shot. The atmosphere was electric and invoked a sense of community.

Nine boys competed in the 10 year old category. They introduced themselves to each other and while shooting, cheered. Several boys offered tips on techniques and applauded the others' successes. Clearly some boys were better than others, but all remained until the end of the tournament to see who had won, if nothing else, but to give their respect to their peers in competition. Such class and social grace was what was fostered by the Knights of Columbus for children, the community, and the school. Make no mistake; this was an investment in the present, which will pay huge dividends in the future.

Competition in our world has taken on an ugly face which has as its main tenet: success by all means possible. The Knights of Columbus Free Throw Tournament challenged these assumptions and replaced them with a spirit of healthy competition rooted in fair play, support, congratulation, and mutual assistance. These values are directly transferable to much of society's behavioural norms. Guiding them should be the role of the Church, school, and the community. The community needs to be led by service organizations such as the Knights of Columbus. We can have a direct and significant effect on the nature of competition and service by offering counter-cultural initiatives like the Free Throw Event, that operate in the realm of 'the popular', but challenge mainstream ideas of competition and winning.

A young lady arrived and began shooting at the net. She was prepared and supported by all of her friends. Once in a while, her gaze would reach over to the assembled crowd. Observing this I looked for her mother or teacher, but to my pleasant surprise she was looking at her father. Dads have it tough these days. They are often working long hours and because the economy is unstable, they are regularly working during times that are important to their children such as recitals, presentations, and sporting events. They also find themselves in less than ideal marital situations, where access and time to children is restricted. Thus, the more community and social opportunities for children that exist, the more occasions in which fathers can spend time with their children in the 21st Century. For fathers who have this luxury, providing those within the fraternity of the fatherhood with more opportunities for time with their children is priceless.

The definition of masculinity needs an overhaul. It has become the purview of flawed athletes, the excessive lifestyles of some popular musicians, and the emasculating messages of mass consumerism. However, there exists a silent, confident form of masculinity that is fostered by the Knights of Columbus and is quite palpable at such events like the Free Throw. The Knights offer moments for parenting and the imparting of true masculine values toward both genders. The Free Throw Tournament fosters such notions as sportsmanship such as: the combined use of physical strength and the wisdom required to wield it, the notion that winning and loosing are both virtuous experiences not to be diluted through some sense of political correctness where competition is nullified, and explicit and implicit means to accept responsibility and encourage masculine respect.

It is the charge of the Knights to make an event like the Free Throw and others, exceptional, extraordinary, and meaningful. They know the importance and effect of these functions upon the family, youth, and our responsibility to offer a type of masculinity that is a viable and stronger alternative to that of secular and pop-cultural notions. It has become quite clear that as the family is inundated with false messages of what family time and recreation are, we must present an alternative that is engaging, and counters selfishness, while redefining success and fair play.

The young man eventually packed up his shoes after the end of the tournament. He didn't win, but stayed until the end. His mother held the shoe box and he took a few more shots at the net. The father with two jobs took a group photo of all the winners and of his sons' competitors; he rushed off to work placing his son in the care of one of his teachers. The young lady held her winning medal in her hand and with the other, her father's hand. They both left well after the competition concluded, after sharing some hoop shots of their own. As for me, I was tired, but I kept the school open and the lights on for a little while longer. I kept them on for the boy with the new shoes, for the son whose working father suddenly decided to be a little late so they could play, and for the young lady and her dad so a few more pictures could be taken. I also kept them on for hope. Hope that I had seen in a new box of shoes and in the work of the Knights of Columbus.

A Casting Call for the Ages

I am not sure what the loneliness of one's golden years would be like, but I can only empathize through an understanding of life's situations. It must be a combination and magnification of the feelings associated with being picked last for a team by one's peers, saying good-bye to family at an airport and realizing how alone you are, and moving out of your parent's home for the first time, then sitting in your new place, by yourself. The one defining difference would be that "the cavalry" was not far off, and by virtue of one phone call, email, or social media contact; the specter of loneliness could be dispelled. This was also made possible by the magic of youth. It is fascinating that upon looking at families in non-western cultures, that perhaps this loneliness is not a factor. We value independence of all stripes and to a degree, individualism, but what have we given up? Does our "teaching career" as parents end with loneliness because of the paradox of success?

One of the reasons people get married and have children is to share their life, love, and experiences. Personal growth, whether through loss or victory is so much more enhanced through sharing and mirroring our reflection in others. I will always remember the global conflicts of the 1990's, not for having been in them, but for hearing them all the way down the street as I neared my home. My grandmother would have the television set on far passed the legendary 11, that one novelty rock act much touted during the same era. Television was a respite for her while my sister and I were at university, and my mother was working. However, I can recall that once we were home, there was much in the way of conversation for the remainder of the afternoon and evening. My grandmother would love to hear our stories, trials and tribulations from the day that passed, and offered a sympathetic ear to our problems. She probably thought about them during the day and prepared answers for us in the evening. None-the-less, she was engaged in our lives and this gave her tremendous purpose. I had seen her grow old and witnessed the limitations of age take away the things she loved. As it gripped her in its unyielding embrace, my grandmother's sense of being became more restricted. She could no longer walk to Church, the scourge of arthritis took away her love of sewing (she had been a seamstress for some of her adult life), then the "World's Greatest Cook" (who never let me into her kitchen) ceded that territory to all of us because she could not stand any longer, and finally, her whit and advice carried toward the end.

Shakespeare once wrote, "All the world is a stage, and all the men and women merely players," he could have added, "And for when that stage clears, we are but left to hear the echo of the audience." As the spirit of the age moves forward, it leaves the elderly in its wake. Their self-perceived context in the world is diminished by older understandings and perceptions of aspects of the economy, politics, religion, and society. While the generous of heart and the wise would regard this as invaluable experience, the commodified and hurried society of the West, views it as fractured social obsolescence. It is the audience that brings hope and meaning. When time has smashed all of life's mirrors and our audience is gone, it is important that we do not become the audience for inanimate entertainment. Living is acting, relating, discussing, loving, and feeling. So it is with this notion that the sudden casting call of youth is required in senior's residences. Oh to have the audience again, even for a short time; to retell the stories and times of my life, to relate to youth is to speak to the future. When Northmount's boys sweep into Leisure World, the infamy of the blaring television set and the stale hours are dispelled. No doubt, the day will come when our own audience is completely gone. I would like to think that instead of gazing out into an empty theatre of life, I would hear a lone clapping sound emanating from the isles, echoing one last, great review, "Well done, my good and faithful servant."

Can we become Superman?

"You will travel far, my little Kal-El, but we will never leave you-even in the face of our deaths. You will make my strength your own. You will see my life through your eyes, as your life will be seen through mine. The son becomes the father. And the father, the son".—<u>Superman,</u> 2006

You see his face in most school photos. You see his face in most school photos. The healthy young man engaged in his studies, speaking with his friends, triumphant in athletics, or raising his hand because he knows the answer. On display for the whole world is an intrinsic quality that cannot be found in any curriculum document or benchmarked competency on a summative assessment, that characteristic is the embodiment of a quiet and noble confidence. The promise of this modern armor is one that is made to every parent that has looked at a kaleidoscope of educational videos and images. We project our child's future on to this positive senior vision. Then we ask ourselves, what do we wish for our sons? Success, love, guidance by a moral compass, and in the distant future; becoming a father and family man, are amongst our laudable goals.

So how do we have him arrive at this state? We begin as all great teachers of male-centered pedagogy would through example and modeling the aforementioned aspirations. Young men will emulate what they see. Patterns of behaviour, social consciousness, notions of charity and empathy, and self-identified concepts of masculinity will be reconciled constantly in a boy's mind. He will imprint upon himself the exemplars of how he will define who he is. If we wish him to be a devoted father and family man, we must show him what that looks like. Not all children have the blessing of an interested and engaged father being with them, or even in the picture all-together.

While we must not acquiesce the male adult role model role solely to the schools; they do however, unquestionably factor in to the process of forging a boy's character. I will often tell parents that the development of a young man is a series of static months and years, followed by "epiphany" type events which set the stage for a higher level of performance, but again along a new plain of static achievement until the next intellectual and evolutionary jump. Another analogy would be the process of looking at an oil painting too closely (a blur); but rather stepping back seeing the details of change over longer periods of time. The acquisition of quiet confidence is the formation, reconciliation, interpretation, and self-identification of male centered traits from the higher order of virtue, over a long period of time. These attributes include: faith, camaraderie, a work ethic, sacrifice, fortitude/courage, perseverance, and holding true to one's convictions. The impact of having a male teacher, further adds to this transfer of ideals. It is not surprising that one of the initial questions in the admissions process surrounds the gender of the teacher for the would-be student.

Teaching fatherhood and what the adult should be is a long journey that does not even end when one actually becomes a father. It is an evolving persona where we must accept failure and success, but all through the eyes of humility and reflection. The noble masculine virtues never are embodied in one man entirely. Much like those moments of epiphany, we can be superman through direct example or deed; thus, creating another mirror for emerging male youth to view themselves. Every young man has the potential to be that superman, if not for just one moment in time. Like the analogy of the oil painting, listen and look for the emergence of virtuous masculinity, cue the iconic John Williams anthem, and watch as the quiet confidence of youth becomes the guiding hand of the father. The son becomes the father . . .

Where has the Time Gone?

I can recall entering Northmount School as a new teacher in 1999, and in awe of the professionals that were presently teaching at the school. Many of these teachers had years, if not decades, more experience than my paltry forty-eight months. What was evident was their willingness to help a new teacher through the slings and arrows of his first full-time year. Mr. Bill Harford, who was Northmount's first principal during the 1990's, was approaching retirement by the time I had arrived, and had encouraged me to teach elementary school instead of secondary, as he felt the latter required a distance of age and a larger bailiwick of resources. His dedication and work ethic were marvels to behold. Mr. Pereira, the director of the school always shared his tremendous sense of humor and wisdom regarding education and schools. He often gave me insights into the most fascinating aspect of Northmount School, its students. The beauty of Mr. Pereira's and Mr. Harford's acumen regarding human relationships is perhaps what I hold most true from that earlier era, and as such, their imparting of knowledge has turned to wisdom through time. It is these human relationships that are at the heart of a school like Northmount. Our school exists in the past, present, and future. As students come and go, they do imprint on the teachers and the institution. This community of memory ebbs and flows through time as memories are evaluated and revaluated against the context of their time and breadth of experiences. Our alumni do one thing that many elementary schools would be hard pressed to proclaim, they come back!

A teacher's greatest rewards have nothing to do with monetary remuneration or holidays, and while those are important aspects of the profession, the enduring wisdom and relationships are what strikes a clear division between the terms job and profession, and profession and vocation. I can recall reading a passage from *Chicken Soup for the Teacher's Soul*, where it presented the quote, "Our vocation is one where we are permitted to work in the future and with the future." We have alumni returning to Northmount at all stages of their lives. The recent graduate comes to share his sense of success, the boys who have left return to catch-up with old acquaintances and see what has changed, the university student has the wisdom to comment upon the effect of his foundation, which has had in helping him construct a multiple level success model, and now the post-secondary student returns to survey that same foundation from the lofty heights of his meaningful career. There have also been a handful of times where parents of former students and alumni themselves have turned to the compassionate and personal nature of the advisory system and reached out for aid, advice, and advocacy with the myriad of problems, personal, professional, and academic that required help in remedying from a trusted voice of the past. As we say at graduation, "Our doors are always open to you."

The achievements of our sons and students make us proud as they develop into the men we all work with them on becoming, this is the present. The Northmount ethos is now mirrored for our present students by the fruition of its promise through our returning alumni. One of my first assignments at the school was teaching Computer Science. It was basic programming and keyboarding. About four years ago, a young man who was one of my first students called and said, "Mr. von Vulte, do you remember me? My name is Ryan, you inspired me to keep going with computers, I thought I would call you, I just finished university and today is the first day of my new job." Working through a lump in my throat and perhaps some suddenly unclear vision, I responded, "Yes I do and where has the time gone?"

Back to School:
A Time for Spiritual Renewal

Advertisers have recently picked-up upon a theme teachers have known about for time-in-memorial. Labor Day is indeed the "real" New Year's Eve. Many young people and adults make new resolutions to do better and to achieve certain goals. Others will choose a new career, or again get serious with their lives. Promises in the calendar year are often linked to the new school year, revolving around our relationship with others, the community, the Church, and God. They often begin with the words, "This year, I am finally going to . . . ." Well, what exactly are you promising to do?

Aside from the laudable academic goals of students, they also question their place within the community and their approach to spiritual goals. This is especially true of children preparing for the Sacraments of the Eucharist, Reconciliation, and Confirmation. Many young boys and girls recognize that they will be taking a further step forward in their Faith accompanied by a progression in age and grade level. Children do not often gaze into the future save for answering the question of what they wish to be in life. The first day of school is special for them because it is one of those opportunities where this is possible. Granted some count the days to Thanksgiving and Christmas, but none-the-less; focus on a new year. The spiritual renewal for children is time and again found through their re-acquaintance with daily prayer and religious studies as well as a ***Catholic atmosphere to witness and learn their Faith***. A factor lost on the supporters of the one-system educational format in Ontario.

Parents whose children are beginning school for the first time, or have had trouble in the past, or are leaving home for university often come by way of spiritual renewal through a wholly different paradigm. One can observe a slight spike in Mass attendance on the Labor Weekend even though it is traditionally the last weekend of summer. There is something quite spiritual about receiving the Lord's blessing before that daunting first day of school. Parents will comment that it does indeed set the tone for their family and themselves for the academic year. Other adults will finally face the empty nest scenario, if but for a day or those with an older brood for an entire year. It is no coincidence that this period of time is the opening of many Council of Parish Service meetings and the recruitment season for such organizations as The Knights of Columbus, The Catholic Women's League, The Legion of Mary, and many others. A tremendous amount of Catholic parents who finally have their heavenly peace and quiet, suddenly seek out and join these groups. It's amazing that this "new year" can bring about feelings of commitment to Church and community.

God asks Catholics to take time to reflect on our spiritual lives, and our covenant and relationship with Him. A sudden shift in season also tends to bring a great deal of anticipation, anxiety, hope, and dread. It is an excellent time to rededicate our prayer lives, and to somehow enhance our friendship and time with Christ, while being more like him in prayer and practice. This "Second New Year's Eve" is so much better than the one in December as it often is more spiritual and possible to keep to our resolutions because we have Christ reminding us on a daily basis. Thus, a Happy New Year to you! May Christ be a large part of it and repeat to you in prayer, the question of what are you going to do?

Preparing for September:
Learning Resolutions become
Academic Revolutions

A good friend and mentor of mine once said that greeting the new school year should be met with the familiar words, "Happy New Year!" This is a truism for all teachers, students, and their respective families. As professionals, we often resolve to further enhance aspects of our practice upon the much needed reflection of the summer break. However, what we often might overlook is transferring some of that reflection and wisdom to our constituent families who are also gearing up for a brand new year. For students, September brings new hope, optimism, and a desire to do better than the previous year. The challenge for parents and teachers is to keep the flame of desire and positivity lit longer than the euphoria of the "honeymoon" period, which is usually three weeks; then the old habits return as adjustment changes into comfort, and comfort becomes complacency. The following are some suggestions for academic success, which I have gleaned in my last fifteen years of teaching that, have proven to be sure fire winners for students and their families:

Mount a cork board of schedules and achievements. Having schedules of activities posted in a visible place begins to instruct the entire family in time management. Due dates for everyone's tests, assignments, and projects should be displayed there as well as sporting and other extracurricular events. Weekend family obligations also need to be posted. Observing due dates keeps them foremost in thought, promotes accountability, and rewards success.

Conduct a weekend binder check. One of the things that drives parents around the bend is when it comes to assisting their children in studying they look at their child's binder and are shocked by the level of disorganization and general appearance of the binder and its contents. This tip is valuable for students from the third grade right to the end of university. For elementary and secondary school students, look through the "Big Five" (English, Mathematics, Science, Social Studies, and French) binders each weekend, review the week, and reorganize, if need be.

Have a family presentation day. Students can truly excel under the twin processes of *retelling* and *gradual release*. The former allows the child to reteach the lesson or experiment to someone else, therefore making that import leap from knowledge and understanding to the higher level of application and analysis. The latter permits your child to take more responsibility for their learning, internalizing it, applying it, and then through emulation, rebroadcasting the knowledge. These sessions can also be quite amusing as students will seek to imitate their teachers. Parents should moderate the level of respect, but keep in mind that imitation is the highest form of flattery.

Establish desk rules and room settings. When children are told to go to their rooms it is often not a punishment for them as all sorts of amusements, electronic and otherwise, can be found there. The immediate work station for an elementary student should be simple, uncluttered, and void of any distractions. Some parents will have a summer and school year configuration for their child's room. Just like diets and resolutions, don't go completely cold turkey. Speak with your child and establish parameters for their electronic media and its terms and times of use. Reserve for yourself the decisions regarding consequences for infractions, remembering that you are the parent.

Create a bag departure zone. One of the things that frustrates busy parents is the morning departure. Making lunches, packing bags, being prepared, and leaving on time, can be an exercise in extreme stress and teeth gnashing frustration. For students, it initiates a day that has already gone wrong. Purchase some plastic or wooden bins (for multiple children, different colours), place them by the door and insist that when the homework period is finished knapsacks must be repacked and placed there before bed. The difference will be palpable!

Build an achieving family dynamic. This can be challenging, especially if a parent has a career that is physically and mentally draining (aren't they all). Our immediate desire when we arrive home is to change into more comfortable clothing, and then hit the couch, while insisting that junior finishes his homework in various octaves of speech. Try changing the format of the evening into the following four identifiable time zones where every family member equally participates: **relaxation and decompression** (unstructured play and athletic time), **dinner preparation and meal time**, followed by a **work period** (for adults reading or preparing for the next day) and finally, some more **relaxation/family time**, perhaps shared reading, and time for the parent(s) to look over homework.

Support your children's teacher and school. As parents we can all espouse the Quebecois phrase, "Je me Souviens" or "I remember." Regardless of our own negative or positive history with education, we must remember to moderate these tales. Parents must avoid an issue that is currently poisoning the culture of education, the unequivocal taking the side of the student against the teacher. Parents must work in partnership with their children's teacher and school, mirroring the standards of the school in the home, and vice-a-versa. All **adult** stakeholders must effectively communicate with each other and work out issues amongst **the adults. Aside from the tenet of the interested parent, this is the second most important factor in student achievement.** Once children and adolescents have witnessed tangible breaches in their perceived adult alliance, all efforts in the home and school will be compromised, if not destroyed. Parents, who believe they are teaching their children assertiveness and agency by engaging in this practice, will one day ask themselves why their adolescent child frequently disobeys them, makes poor choices, and refuses to listen. The answer is quite simple; you have made them your equal.

I have heard it said from a parent who was in commerce, that each child is like their own corporation and business is booming. The commencement of the school year is much like baseball's spring training or the grand opening of a business; hope springs eternal. Our children have new clothes, school supplies, and wishes for a great year. We make resolutions with them and invigorate them with positivity. Much like New Year's resolutions and their accompanying gym memberships, learning resolutions require long-term strategies that will avoid failure and truly become academic revolutions!

Edwards Brothers Malloy
Oxnard, CA USA
January 31, 2014